Fred Gleeck

SELL YOUR BRAIN POWER

Information Marketing in 7 Easy Steps

Fast Forward Press

Las Vegas • New York • Los Angeles

Publisher's Cataloging-In-Publication Data
(Prepared by The Donohue Group, Inc.)

Gleeck, Fred.
  Sell your brain power: information marketing in 7 easy steps / Fred Gleeck.

    p. ; cm.

  ISBN: 978-0-936965-99-4

  1. New products. 2. Marketing--Planning. 3. Business--Planning. I. Title.

TS170 .G54 2010
658.5752   2010928019

ISBN: 978-0-936965-99-4

First published in 2012

Published by Fast Forward Press/FG Productions, inc.
209 South Stephanie Street, Suite B-209, Henderson, NV 89012

Interior layout: Nick Zelinger, www.nzgraphics.com

Publisher's Note:
This publication is designed to provide accurate and authoritative information in regard to the subject matter covered. It is sold with the understanding that the publisher is not engaged in rendering legal, accounting or other professional services. If you require legal advice or other expert guidance, you should seek the services of a competent professional.

Contents

About the Author

My name is Fred Gleeck and I wrote this book. Whenever I read a book I'm always curious about the author. I'm interested in learning a little about them both personally and professionally, so . . . I'll give you what I'd expect to receive.

I was born in Japan and raised in the Philippine Islands. My Dad was an American Diplomat. As a kid growing up in the Philippines, my goal was to play professional golf. Although I won a couple of Junior golf championships, I wasn't close to as good as you need to be to play golf competitively in the U.S.

I left Manila just before I turned 18 to go to college in the United States. I briefly attended Wake Forest University before moving to the University of Florida in Gainesville (GO GATORS!). While there I studied marketing and psychology. I graduated with enough credits for degrees in both.

I wanted to study theatre, but my parents told me that if I chose that major I'd have to pay for college myself. They told me they would finance my education if I studied business, so that's what I did.

I then went to Glendale, Arizona to get a Masters Degree in International management. The name of the school is Thunderbird. Not to be confused with the "fine wine" by the same name. I graduated with a Masters Degree in International Management.

In 1979, immediately after leaving graduate school, I read a book called: "Put Your Money Where Your Mouth Is!" (by Robert Anthony – now out of print). It showed you how you could make a living as a professional speaker. This seemed like a great way to combine my theatrical interest with my business background academically. But . . . first a foray into corporate life!

After finishing my Masters I moved to New York City where I was promptly fired by 5 major corporations in a row. There seemed to be unanimous agreement I should be self-employed.

In the early 80s I was mentored by a guy named Howard Shenson. He was an expert in both seminar marketing and consulting. I worked with him for a couple of years, attending many of his events and working with him one-on-one. We also got to be friends.

In 1984, soon after leaving my last corporate job, I gave my first "open to the public" seminar just outside of New York City in Saddlebrook, NJ. I made some decent money and enjoyed the process of marketing and promoting my own seminars and events.

Before doing that first event I had already developed a couple of my own audio products. I developed my own products because I had watched the really successful professional speakers. They ALL had a LOT of "stuff" that they sold from the back of the room.

I decided to use them as my model.

Between 1984 and now I have produced over 4,000 hours of audio and video products for myself and my clients. I also produced one of the first infomercials selling information products back in 1985.

I now own over 600 domain names and I've developed extensive product lines for a slew of niche markets. Niches that range from self-storage to catering to video producers and limousine drivers.

In addition to my own niche markets, I now spend a lot of time working with a highly select group of clients to help THEM develop, create and market THEIR information products both on and offline.

Why should you follow my advice on the topic of information product marketing?

I feel that I have the RIGHT to author a book on this topic because I've done it myself. I have not, nor will I claim to have made, a bazillion dollars in this business. AND, as opposed to many of my peers, I don't think lying makes sense.

I WILL boldly make the claim that I teach info product marketing BETTER than ANYONE else out there. If you're looking for a simple, easy to follow system, this is it. And humbly, I believe I'm the guy to teach you that system!

Website Addresses

Any websites that I reference will not have the "www," In front of it. Everyone knows this convention, so I chose to leave it out when referencing web addresses.

This Book is ALREADY Out of Date

Even if you were the first person to buy this book, it would already be out of date. The internet-based information marketing business is constantly changing. Given that fact, immediately after putting information into print there may be errors, or things that need to be updated.

I've figured out a way to combat this problem.

Go to my website, FredGleeck.com. Click on the BOOK image. You'll find this book. Clicking on the book will have any updates or changes since the last publication date of the book. So, if you find something that is inaccurate, or a link that doesn't work, please contact me at: gleeckfred@gmail.com.

In the subject line please put the words: "BOOK ERROR" and I'll make sure and make the changes on the site AND send YOU a SMALL gift for helping out.

This applies to typos as well.

The site will also give you the latest information in the field of information marketing. If there any changes to anything important, you'll find it on the site. Check it regularly for updates and "freebies".

FREE OFFER

Find out more about the author
by visiting FredGleeck.com

AND to get your FREE
Information Marketing
Audio Course
(worth $397),
go to http://goo.gl/VeClB

FREE OFFER

Chapter 1
Introduction

Introduction

This book is all about HOW to create and market your own information products. When I use the term "Sell Your Brain Power" it may be a bit misleading. The information products that you sell don't have to be about topics that you already know about. BUT, I suggest you START there. Once you understand the process, it will be easy to repeat the steps with topics you may not KNOW, but have decided to work on for whatever reason.

What I've put together for you here is a SYSTEM. This system will work BEST when you follow the steps in the order I've provided for you. If you try and "freelance" and do things your own way when you first get started, your chances for success will be MUCH reduced.

Even if you're a highly intelligent individual (and I expect you are since you bought this book! – LOL), you'll be tempted to do things a different way. YOUR way. I ask that you don't. Not initially. When you get started, stick to the system that I've created for you. After you've perfected MY system, if you want to start improvising at that point, be my guest.

What Is an Information Product?

An information product is any product or service that provides people with knowledge and information about a specific topic. "Info products" as they are often called are produced in a number of forms. They can be written, audio, video, experiential or even software.

They include but are not limited to, books, e-books, CD ROMs, audios, mp3s, downloadable audio files, videos, DVDs, downloadable videos, screen capture videos, seminars, membership sites, tele-seminars, webinars, coaching, or consulting. Any kind of information that you can sell in ANY form. It's a catch-all term that covers a large number of possible options. Remember, when I use the term PRODUCT, I use it loosely. In this book, I'll use the word to refer to EITHER a product or a service.

Timely vs. Timeless Products

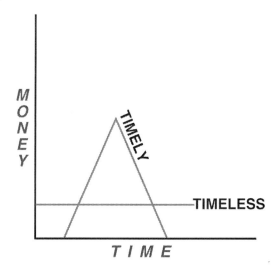

There are two basic types of info products. I call them TIMELY or TIMELESS. Timely products are those which take advantage of a trend, or relate to issues that are only relevant NOW or for a relatively short window of time.

Any product related to internet marketing would be timely. Why? Because the information is constantly changing. That being said, you can make a LOT of money selling timely products. And I suggest you do!

Timeless products are those that are the same yesterday, today and tomorrow. The best example of a timeless info product is a song. Another example would be a book like "Think and Grow Rich". Both a song (if it's good) and that book will have relevance many years from now.

Which types of products should YOU produce? (TRICK question alert)

The answer: BOTH!

Timely products will give you a BURST of money for a relatively short period of time. Timeless products will bring you small, consistent profits virtually forever. IF you do things right! I'll be showing you how to do both.

Why Sell Info Products?

I've been selling info products for over a quarter of a century. I think it's a great business and highly recommend you do the same. For me, there are some very simple, rational reasons for YOU to get involved selling information. Here they are:

Low Start-Up Cost

For less than $3,000 the first year, and then less than $2,000 every year after that, it's hard to find any business that you can start and run for less.

Live Anywhere

You can live anywhere you want. Since virtually everything you have to do can be done on-line, it's your choice as to where you want to base yourself.

Good Money

You can make a lot of money. If you want to do it honestly, it won't happen overnight, but it is possible to make VERY good, VERY big money, over time.

High Margins

Most businesses are ecstatic if they can get 50% margins. Just ask Walmart! In the info products business you can make something for $1 and sell it for $100. In many cases you can make it for LESS than $1 and sell it for MORE than $100.

Make Money While You Sleep

Properly set up, your web-based info products business will allow you to make money day and night. While you're sleeping in Boston, a gal in Australia can be buying your ebook in Melbourne. The money will be deposited into your checking account before you get up.

Build it Once, Make Money Forever

With info products, once you create a product, you could be making money on it 20 or 30 years from now. This is very possible with what I referred to earlier as a "timeless" product.

Makes YOU an Expert in Your Field

Once you've started to create info products in your topic area, you'll gain notoriety. With this fame will come all sorts of opportunities, not least of which are speaking opportunities.

Travel

If you like to travel, you can do so with this business. Not long ago, I took a trip to Europe. When I came back I had more money in the bank than before I left. Even accounting for the money I spent on the trip.

Virtually NO Delivery Issues

As internet connection speeds increase, more and more products will be deliverable over the web. Videos have always been a problem because of the size of the files. As transmission speeds increase, this will no longer be an issue. Soon, EVERY info product will be web deliverable.

Conclusion

If this sounds good to you, then you're not far from getting going with your own information marketing business. But, don't let me kid you, this is not a GET RICH QUICK business. You will hear this from other so-called "gurus" in the field. They are LYING to you. Every business takes time, effort and energy. But, if you are willing to put in the time, you'll be well rewarded.

Chapter 2
Things to Remember BEFORE You Start

Introduction

In this chapter I'd like to give you some of my ideas about how this business really works. These items are really about the mindset you need to have to be successful in the field of information marketing. Read and think about each one of them.

Measurement Eliminates Argument

The information products business is all about numbers. Feelings are fine, but they can't be measured. To make sure you are making the right decisions, you need to quantify everything you possibly can. Make sure that anything in your information marketing business that can be measured is tracked. Without data, good decisions are impossible.

Done is Better Than Perfect

I use this line in every seminar or speech that I do regarding information products. If you spend all your time trying to make a product perfect, it will NEVER get made. It's like the writer you know who has been writing the great American novel for the past 12 years. He's trying to make it perfect and as a result, it NEVER gets done.

The nice thing about info products is that they can ALWAYS be REDONE. Don't misunderstand me. I'm not saying you should produce CRAPPY products. Hardly! What I am saying is that if you are producing great information, stop dwelling on things that really aren't important to your buyers. I'm talking here about how the product looks.

If your product looks REALLY slick, it may actually be perceived as less valuable (I'll explain this in the next section). Additionally, if you want to spend a lot of time editing, you won't be making any money selling the product. It won't be available to sell.

If you're not completely happy with the product you produce, get it out there and start making money. Then spend some time to make it BETTER as soon as you can. This assumes that you are releasing products that have GREAT content but may need a bit of "cleaning up" in some other area(s).

On the editing front, I myself do NO editing. When one of my dogs barks when I'm doing a recording, it stays in. I also spend virtually no time on packaging. The vast majority of people who buy my products are simply interested in how to do things. They could care less what the packaging looks like. And since the ultimate determinant of success in this business is whether people buy from you again, it hasn't caused me any major problems.

The critical point to remember is this: People will ALWAYS forgive poor production quality, they will NEVER forgive poor content!

Understand that YOUR situation may be different. IF you deal with corporate clients or folks in the entertainment field, you may need to spend time on "fancy" packaging. BUT, this is the exception and not the rule.

Sell Free as Hard as You Sell Paid

What you give away for free is critically important to your success in the information marketing business. When people visit your site for the first time, they will be skeptical. Although your primary goal is to sell them something, the vast majority won't buy on their first visit.

Your next goal if they don't buy is to get them to opt-in to your list. You do this by "seducing" them with a great free offer. This free offer may be an audio, a pdf report or even a video. Whatever it is, the key to getting them to agree to get the free information is the TITLE you use to promote it. If you're using a video to try and get them to sample your material that will be critical as well. But the title is critical to get people to take action.

The quality of the free material you offer is vitally important, but at this point, they haven't seen or heard it yet, so how you promote it becomes the MOST important thing.

Selling your FREE offer is as, or more important, as what you are actually selling. A small number of highly successful sites close 5% of visitors on making a purchase. This leaves 95% of the people who don't buy. The SALE you make to get them to opt-in to your list allows you the opportunity to sell them in the future. By giving them something of real value for free you build their trust in hopes of selling them something later.

This is why you need to sell your FREE offer as hard as you sell your PAID products.

I've seen people use multi-page sales letters just to get a larger percentage of people to sign up for your list. I give away e-books (FredGleeck.com/ebooks). The price for the books in physical form is over $100. Why not download them yourself now?

Make sure that YOU give away free material that is of true value. Make sure that after they get the material they feel they would have been willing to PAY for it.

It's got to be that good.

Handling Returns

I don't handle returns well. I know my products are good and take it personally when people ask for refunds. This is an area where you should NOT follow my lead. Returns are a fact of life in the information marketing business. Get used to them. Try NOT to take it personally. Trust me, I'm STILL trying after many years.

IF you have people who work for you, this would be a great place to use them. Get someone OTHER than yourself to politely respond to all refund requests. Give them their money back and send them on their way.

Depending on HOW they ask for a refund, it MAY make sense to block them (using WebMarketingMagic.com) from ordering again from you. Don't try and keep customers who are mean or nasty. They are NOT the kind of people you want in your database. You also don't want to allow people to KEEP buying who have asked for refunds more than ONCE. Those folks should definitely be blocked from placing future orders.

Don't Believe Anyone's Numbers But Your Own

There are a lot of LIARS out there in info marketing field. When you hear people throwing around big numbers, don't get discouraged. Much of what they say is complete and total HOGWASH.

Track and believe only your own numbers. You need to track them, but only concern yourself with whether yours are moving in the right direction. Don't try and do any comparing to others. It won't help, and it's not relevant to your success.

Joint Venture Deals

Many years ago, I sat down for lunch with another of the well-known "gurus" in this industry. He's a household name that anyone who in the field would know. The portion of the conversation that I remember most revolved around revenue splits with joint venture partners.

My contention was that I try and make EVERY deal I do a 50-50 deal. That way, both parties feel equal. Neither party feels as if they are working for the other. Mr. "X" on the other side of the table thought I was nuts. He contended that there are numerous situations in which a NON 50-50 deal makes sense.

He's right.

I just don't want to run my business with people who don't feel like they are equal "partners" with me in a venture. When I don't feel a deal is equal, I try and structure the workload and responsibilities in such a way as to MAKE it an equal deal.

But, that being said, you may want to run your business differently than I do mine. It's your choice but that's the way I see things.

Ethical Considerations in Information Product Marketing

If you want to make a lot of money quickly, please skip this section. If you want to make a career for yourself in the info product business, then keep reading.

I think it's a universal fact that you can make MORE money if you "bend the truth" to suit your needs. Lie about your numbers. Embellish a story. All of it will help you to sell more products and services, AND make more money. SHORT TERM.

Integrity is one of those things that's either black or white. As my Mom used to say, you can't be a "little bit pregnant." The same is true with honesty and integrity.

I could say this more delicately, but it's not my nature. There are a lot of CROOKS in this business. I can't name names. My lawyer won't let me. But, I will tell you that I will only partner with a VERY small number of people. This is because I only want to work with people where I can be 100% certain of their honesty and integrity.

What does this mean for you?

It means that you MUST be careful. Make sure and do your due diligence before doing any business with people in this field. If you make the WRONG choices it will reflect VERY poorly on you and severely hurt your reputation. Don't believe their claims. Ask for proof. Don't buy into the hype no matter how big or well known the guru. Only believe your OWN numbers!

I get offers daily to do joint ventures and/or speak at someone's event or seminar. I turn down just about all of them. Why?

NO sum of money is worth sacrificing your reputation for. 'Nuf said.

Sell Your Customers Crack!!!

Whenever I speak to a group, I always use the following illustration to make a very important point. I tell people that I own a site called CrackDealerMarketing.com. There is nothing there at the moment. It's a place-holder for a future site on this topic.

Immediately after telling them about the site I then ask: "How many crack dealers are in the room today?" I usually get a couple of people who raise their hands (I doubt that's their real profession).

I then say: "How does a crack dealer do business? The answer?

First they give people free or reduced priced samples. After they get them hooked, they have customers for life. And at a price that they can set . . . with NO objections.

If you can find something to sell to your niche that they MUST have, you're in good shape. Sell people an indispensable product and your reorder rates go to virtually 100%.

YOU need to find products and services that are like CRACK. Sell that crack to your niche market.

The "10 Times" Rule

Every time I create a product of any kind, I ask myself this simple question: "After people use this product, will they feel like it's worth 10 times more than what they paid?"

If the answer is NO, I go back and redo the product.

If you create products that people feel are worth MUCH more than what you ask people to pay, you'll be in GREAT shape. People will keep ordering MORE from you and your return rates will be extremely low.

The Value Equation

People always ask me at seminars and events how they should price their products. The value of a product and what you should charge for it is NOT based on the product cost. It's based on the VALUE you deliver with that product. The SYSTEM you learn in this book is worth a TON more than the $20 or so you paid for it.

In most cases, except for a book, you want to charge based on the value you deliver. This is NOT true with books because people have a "mental set" about what the price of a book should be. Although, I HAVE seen a book of around 200 pages sell for close to $300. In that example, the person was using the value equation to price the book.

If you want to know how to price a given product, START with the value equation. Then make adjustments accordingly.

Doing it "Your Own Way"

I was on the web pretty early on. I started going to internet marketing seminars in the late 1990s. Soon thereafter, I was speaking at those same events. Now, I do almost exclusively my OWN events. Why?

Because I don't want to be associated with many of the folks I used to work with. They just don't seem to care about ethical behavior. Sometimes in business, as in life, you just have to do it YOUR way.

For me that means forgoing a lot of cash and running as ethical a business as I possibly can. I suggest you listen to your conscience and do the same. In the LONG run, you'll be better off.

Handling Difficult People/Customers

Every once in a while, you'll get a NUTCASE who either buys from you or starts to pester you. In any business there are a percentage of people (just like in the general population) who aren't "quite right."

My suggestion is to let them go. If they bought something, refund their money. Then blacklist their IP address (in a system like WebMarketingMagic.com that we'll talk about later it's easy to do). If you're new to the web, it just means that you make it impossible for someone to order from you in the future. Assuming they use the same computer.

When people get NUTTY, I leave. I don't want to have anything to do with them. I suggest you do the same. Don't ever get sucked into that rat hole.

50% of Something vs. 100% of Nothing

A lot of people feel like they have to WIN the negotiating war. I don't. I like to find a way to make SOME money rather than NO money. I try to always find a way to give people MORE than they would expect on a deal.

Why? Because any deal that I can work with another person where I can get a piece of the action works for me! I'd rather make 50% of something than 100% of nothing. I suggest that you adopt the same thinking. Do this and you'll be well ahead of the game.

Keeping this in mind, don't be foolish. There are times when people don't deserve the percentages they might request.

"Gleeckanomics"

This term was coined by my good friend, Avish Parashar. I would always talk about how my goal was to generate 100 checks a month from 100 different sources. Avish heard me say this so much that he coined the term Gleekanomics to describe it.

I would suggest you find a way to run your information marketing business using Gleekanomics. It's always better to have your revenue coming in from a diversified collection of sources rather than just one. Thanks, Avish! I wholeheartedly agree.

People "STEALING" Your ideas

Information marketers are always worried about people STEALING their ideas. If you don't have a well-stocked information funnel, you should be worried. The intelligent info marketer understands that to make really good money you have to have lots of products to sell at a lot of different price points.

If you make sure that your products are packed with bounce back offers, you might even encourage people to "lift" your material. In some of my books I will say something like: "As a registered user of this book you're entitled to the following free bonuses." Someone who has a bootleg copy is now unable to get this promised freebie. Too bad for them! They now have to go back and buy the book.

Also, throughout a book or any product, I will liberally sprinkle suggestions about other products and services where I get paid either directly or indirectly. I suggest you follow my lead here.

Don't concern yourself with policing the theft of your information products. The line I always use is: "Expect people to be dishonest, you'll RARELY be disappointed." Understanding how people ARE, build your info products accordingly. Fill them with bounce back offers and ALWAYS mention your other existing products when you create new products.

Bounce backs get people to BOUNCE BACK to a website or location you send them to within an existing product.

Conclusion

Keep these ideas and concepts in mind as you start and build your information products business. Follow these principles and you'll be able to build a thriving, ethical, info products business. One where you won't have to worry about the Department of Justice coming to visit you.

Chapter 3
Putting Your Systems in Place

Introduction

Like any business, running an information products business requires systems. But, as opposed to a traditional brick and mortar business, they are much less expensive. That being said, there are certain things that you MUST have in place before you get started.

I'll be making a number of recommendations in this section and throughout the rest of this book. Some of these recommendations will be software. Other resources will be people.

I am VERY careful with the people I recommend. There are some very shady operators out there, and I want to help you avoid some of them. No matter whom you use, make sure you check them out thoroughly before you give them a dime. EVEN the people I send your way. It is YOUR responsibility to do your due diligence.

Do it Yourself or Get Help?

This is the first question you need to ask yourself: Are you technically capable of putting up a website and running it? If the answer is NO, then you're going to have to get help. Running an information products business requires you to know, or have access to, knowledge about web related matters.

There is a fair amount to this. Creating the site, making it look good, using WebMarketingMagic.com, uploading your digital products, etc. etc.

If you do need help, then I have some suggestions for you. There are a lot of people who prey on people who want to get started in this business. Early on I was a victim of some incredibly predatory practices that I'm hoping I can help you avoid. Like with any field, you have to be careful.

Technical Help (If you need it)

You can get help on technical web related matters from a variety of sources. I can only recommend one. His name is Dave Hamilton and he bills himself as the WebMarketingMagician.

Dave came up to me at a seminar a number of years back. He introduced himself and said that he would be willing to help my "students" with the technical side of the info products business. I've been working with Dave for years and can recommend him without reservation.

He is a rare combination of both technical talent AND communication skill. A very unusual set of skills to find in one person.

If you need help in setting up your site, or some of the finer points of WebMarketingMagic, he's the guy to turn to. For more information on Dave, go to: WebMarketingMagician.com.

Domain Name Selection/Registration

If you follow my system you'll end up reserving a LOT of domain names. No matter which company you use to reserve them, there are a few key points to keep in mind. First, you want to have ALL of your domain names under one roof. Why? Because they are infinitely easier to manage and you won't risk losing a domain name like I did.

A number of years back I paid $1000 for a domain name. When the domain was put into my name I had to use a domain registrar I had never used before. When my email address changed, I never received notification to renew the name. Net result? I paid $1000 to own a domain name for a year that I NEVER used. Someone else now owns it. Don't let the same thing happen to you.

My suggestion is that you use MY domain reservation company, UltraCheapDomains.com. I set the prices as low as they allow me to and it's as good a deal as you'll get anywhere. By way of full disclosure, I do make about a quarter on every domain you reserve. This does not come out of YOUR pocket, but is the commission I'm given for reselling domain names.

In the event that you see yourself reserving MORE than 50 or 60 domains a year, I would suggest you take a look at: SellDomainsForProfit.com. This site will allow you to set up your own domain reseller account (like UltraCheapDomains.com) and "commission yourself" for every name you reserve. Since there is a yearly fee to maintain this account, it will only make sense if you see yourself owning/reserving more than the 50 or 60 domain names.

Again, I receive a VERY small override for every domain you buy but it does not affect your price or the prices you charge others if you choose to offer domain name registration to people other than yourself.

Hosting Your Site

A hosting company is where your domain "sits". It is a hard drive somewhere out there in cyberspace. In order for a site to be seen on the internet, you need to get a hosting account. This is a mandatory item. Without it, no one will be able to see or find your site.

I am now using a site that you can find at CoolHosting Tool.com. I use it for the majority of my sites. I suggest you do the same. They are very affordable and extremely reliable. Also, all of the free instructional video training that I do revolves around this hosting company. It will be much easier for you to understand the videos if you use them for hosting as well.

Website Creation: 3 Types of Sites You'll Need

Now that you have your domain name and a place to host your site, you'll need to put up the actual site or sites. As an information marketer, it's a good idea for you to have 3 types of sites when you get started. They are the authority site, the sales letter site and the squeeze page site. I highly recommend that you use WordPress for all of these sites.

There will be much more covered in later chapters on this topic, I just want to give you a brief overview here.

WordPress was designed as a blogging platform. Because of its ease of use and set up, many people are now using it as the backbone of their websites. It is FREE and has a large community of developers that support it. If you use CoolHostingTool.com as I suggest, installing it takes just one click.

If you combine WordPress with a good looking "template" you can make your site look VERY professional. The template that I use can be found by going to CoolWordPressTool.com.

In the long run, you'll want to have a separate domain for each and every product or service you sell. If you have 10 products you'll end up with at LEAST 11 sites. Your one authority site and 10 separate Sales Letter sites for each of your 10 products.

Chances are you may also have some Squeeze Page sites as well.

This may sound like a lot but it is NOT. It will help from an SEO (Search Engine Optimization) standpoint and given the prices on domain names and hosting, it makes sense. Trust me on this one. It's what I do. If you followed my advice and had 11 sites, it would cost you under $200 a year for the domain names AND the hosting. Very much worth it.

You will also want to visit AuthoritySites101.com. It's a product that Dave Hamilton put together. It's easy to under-stand and will be invaluable if you're not a technical type.

Authority Site

Setting up an authority site is done for three main reasons. First, to promote you as THE (or one of the), definitive experts in the field. Second is for you to be able to get great SEO rank-ings in your field. Lastly, to capture names and get people to opt-in to your list. For an example of this type of site, please look at: SeminarMarketingExpert.com or FredGleeck.com.

This is where the bulk of your CONTENT should sit. You'll want great feature articles (that are static) and blog posts that you put up regularly. You also want to make sure that you have a very compelling free offer that people would be crazy to pass up.

Take a look at that site and COPY it. It has been very successful for me in accomplishing the three tasks I described above. You should do the same thing for your area of expertise.

Sales Letter Site

Your sales letter sites are set up for one reason. To get people to BUY one of your products or services. It's a simple sales letter (often combined with a video) that you might have seen used on a direct mail piece, but it's online. A sample of this kind of site can be seen at FredInfoBootcamp.com.

The MAIN purpose of a sales letter site is to get people to BUY the product or service you are offering. The secondary purpose is to get those who don't buy to opt-in to your list. After they opt-in, to get them on an auto-responder series and convince them to buy at some point in the future.

Building your database of names via the opt-in procedure as well as auto responders are both functions of WebMarketingMagic.com.

You'll also end up adding other elements to your site as well. Things like audio and video. This will be covered in great detail in the chapter on Conversion.

Squeeze Page Site

Squeeze pages are set up for one purpose only. To get people to give you their email address. As an information marketer, the big picture is to build the largest email list you possibly can. Squeeze page sites will help you do just that.

When you set up a squeeze page, make sure that you have something of VERY high perceived value to give away. It could be an audio file or a PDF report. No matter what it is, it has to be perceived by your potential customers as very valuable. JUST from the title you give it.

As I mentioned earlier, all three of the sites that I recommend that you put together can be done using some of Dave Hamilton's tools.

Google Adwords Account

You will also want to set up a Google Adwords account. This is an account where you can pay Google to get people to visit your site. For many years, this is how information marketers did their testing. It is also used for driving traffic to sites.

Along the top and along the right side after you do a Google search you'll see what are called "sponsored" links. These are ads that people are paying to have appear when someone does a search. They are called pay-per-click ads.

You can do the same. When you get started, this is the best way to drive traffic to your site quickly to test some key numbers.

Set one up your account now, but don't start using it until you are a bit further along.

Host to SERVE Your Audios and Videos

YouTube is great for "public" videos, but you'll need another system for audio and video you want to privately host on your own site. You can get this done by going to CoolStorageTool.com.

When people go to your site and you want them to see a video that's not on a public site like You-Tube, you need a place that "serves" up your video. This means that your video "sits" on their hard drive or server. When people click on the play button, the video plays from that site. This can be expensive if you don't use the right provider.

To make it super easy to use this service, you'll also need a program to upload your audio and video files. Do that by using CoolUploadTool.com. These two tools in combination will make it super easy (and cheap) to host audios and videos on your site.

Membership Sites/Protected Pages

Many information marketers hide certain content that they create and ask people to become "members" in order to see, hear or read that content. The best way to understand this is that every page on your website has a door. In most cases that door is unlocked.

Membership site software allows you to put a lock on the door to a specific page or sets of pages. When visitors have the key, they can get through the door and see the pages. On those pages you can have anything. Videos, audios or text.

There are a lot of different ways to do this. The simplest way I've found is using the same tool I use. You can find it at: CoolMembershipTool.com. You'll be able to set up a basic membership site using this software.

WebMarketingMagic

WebMarketingMagic.com is your one stop solution for all of your back-end systems needs as an information product marketer. It has a large number of tools that any serious information marketer would want to have.

The various tools that are contained under its umbrella ARE available ala carte from other providers. Some of them MAY even be a bit better when looked at in isolation. NONE of them, or any other provider is as good at proving a complete one-stop solution that integrates all of these tools.

The system will cost you around $100 a month and is worth EVERY penny. I'm sorry, but I do not have any other recommendation for a similar solution. Nothing is even comes close.

Here are some of the components of WebMarketing Magic. com and what is does:

Digital Delivery System - People can download digital files for free or for a fee

Ezine Broadcast Module - Lets you stay in regular touch with customers/prospects

Auto-Responder System - Send as many automated messages as you want

Client Management System - Keep a database of your customers and prospects

Affiliate Module - Set people up to sell your products and get paid

Coupon Module - Allows you to set up special "deals" using a coupon system

Tell-A-Friend - Makes it easy for others to refer people your way

Automate Unsubscribe - Avoid SPAM complaints with this automated feature

Ad Trackers - Track the effectiveness of ads you place or links you suggest

Shopping Cart - Make it simple and easy for your customers to buy from you online

Credit Cards - Give your customers a variety of payment options

Merchant Account

A merchant account allows businesses to accept payments by debit or credit cards. A merchant account also serves as an agreement between a retailer, a merchant bank and payment processor for the settlement of credit card and/or debit card transactions. When you sign up for WebMarketingMagic.com you can also sign up to receive a merchant account. This is a mandatory item.

Some new information marketers are choosing to just use Paypal for this function. Do NOT do this. Paypal does not allow you to capture people's email addresses when they buy. Having the email addresses of your buyers is critical to your long term success.

Gateway Account

A gateway account serves at the interface between your merchant account and your WebMarketingMagic.com account. The gateway protects credit card information by encrypting the information. It allows the information to be securely passed between your customers and your merchant account. This is technical computer "stuff" so don't get too worried about it.

Teleseminar Line: FreeConferenceCall.com

If you want to get a group of people on a big "party line" you'll need a teleseminar line. This allows you to hold a conversation (sometimes ONE way) with as many as 1,000 people or more at the same time.

Many organizations use this for sales and training meetings. It allows for LOTS of people to be listening (or interacting) on a phone call. Numerous companies offer this service. Many are free. I suggest you start with one that is free.

Webinar Line

A webinar is very similar to a teleseminar. You can talk to a group of people at the same time and allow them see your computer screen. This is critical when what you are demonstrating something that has a visual or online component. IF what you are teaching to others is even marginally visual, you'll need to get a webinar line.

I have one that I share with others. This helps you to lower your costs unless you need one ALL the time. If you are interested in sharing mine, take a look at FredWebinars.com.

Google Analytics

In order for you to make intelligent business decisions, each site you own should have software to track the 4 key statistics you need to know as an information marketer. You MUST know: 1) the number of unique visitors who come to your site, 2) the percentage of people who buy your product, 3) the number of people who don't buy your product, but opt-in to your list and 4) the average visitor value your site produces.

A unique visitor is one who comes to your site for the first time. If that same person visits your site later in the day, they are NOT counted. If you are selling a $100 digital product and 100 people visit your site, and 4 of them buy, then your closing ratio is 4%.

If 4 out of 100 buy your product, then 96 did not buy. You will also want to know how many of those 96 people decided to opt-in to your list. Let's say that you get 22 people to opt-in to your list, then your closing ratio for opt-ins is 23%.

Going on the assumption that 4 people bought your $100 digital product, then your average visitor value is $4. You generated $400 in revenue and you had 100 visitors. $400 divided by 100 gives you the number $4.

There are some additional numbers that are somewhat important, but these four are critical to your business success.

Google provides you with a free tool to be able to track the important data or "metrics" on your site. When set up, it will be able to tell you the key things you need to know on your site.

All you need is a Gmail account with Google and you'll have access to use the Google Analytic tools.

Hardware

I hate to sound like that typical MAC "freak", but for an information marketer, you NEED a MAC. Keep your PC for other things, but use your new MAC for the creation of information products. Why? Because it's so unbelievably EASY to use.

Going with Apple will allow you to use the iLife and iWork tools to create your info products. I use a program like Pages to put together written products like this book. iTunes is not just great for listening to music, but for helping to create your audio programs. Use Garageband to edit if you like, and then import the file into Itunes to finish up.

Videos couldn't be easier than with iMovie. If you're making more sophisitcated videos, then you may need Final Cut Pro, but for mere mortal info product folks like you and me, iMovie is perfect.

Trust me, once you TRY it, you'll agree. One of the best things about going this route is something that the Apple store will provide you: one on one training. When you buy a new Mac computer, they will add on this service for just $100 a year. This gives you regular access to an EXPERT to train you on the various tools I've talked about here.

Buy the Mac and USE the one-on-one training and you'll be set to produce any and all of your info products. Even if you're a PC person, get a Mac for this purpose.

Screen Capture Software

I am constantly doing something on my computer that I want to demonstrate for others. This software allows me to take a video (and record audio) of what I'm doing at any time on my computer screen. For you as an information marketer, you'll find this tool to be invaluable.

As a Mac owner, I use a program called CoolScreenCapture .com I highly recommend it. If you're a PC user, Camtasia is the program that most people use. My understanding is that it is relatively easy to use as well.

Total Cost for These Systems

Technical Assistance - Less than $1000 (depending on what you need)

Domain Registration - Less than $10 per domain name per year***

Hosting Fees - Less than $100 per year***

WordPress - Free

WordPress Theme - Around $100 flat fee

WebMarketingMagic - Around $100 a month***

Merchant Account - Around $20 per month***

Gateway Account - Around $20 per Month***

Teleseminar Line - Free

Webinar Line - Starting at $25 for a "shared" line

Google Analytics - Free

Screen Capture Software - Around $100 - one time flat fee

***Mandatory Items

Total Cost per Year: $1,750 - $4,000

Conclusion

These are all of the systems you'll need to get going as an information marketer. The total cost for these items is extremely low compared to just about any other type of business you might consider. If they are on the list above, they are necessary for you to succeed in this business. Get going on setting up your systems NOW.

Chapter 4

The Seven Steps to Selling Information Products

Introduction

I've broken down the "system" I teach into seven distinct steps. This will make it easier for you to learn and implement these ideas in a logical order. Each item has numerous subsections, but this is the basic blueprint for success in the information marketing business. I'll explain exactly how to do each of these steps in its own separate chapter. Here's an overview of the system.

Step #1: Decide on a Niche

First you'll need to figure out what group you'll be targeting with your information products. Before you even develop the product you'll need to really understand who you are targeting. You'll also want to make sure that the group you're targeting has an interest in what you'll be selling.

Step #2: Writing the Copy to Sell Your Product

The words, audio and video you use to sell people when they come to your site are crucial to making this business work. The "copy", the words you use to sell, whether in print, audio or in your video are critical to your success.

Step #3: Creating Your Product

After you write the copy, you'll now want to develop your product based on that copy. Write the copy FIRST? Yes. Writing the promotion for your info product will help you design it.

In addition to writing the copy to sell it, you'll have to decide whether the product should be in written, audio, video, or some other form. The answer will depend on what your potential customers would most prefer. Only then should you start producing the product.

Step #4: Designing a Website to Sell Your Product

After your product is done, you'll want to have a website to sell it. Although you may be doing some selling offline, the bulk of your sales will happen online. So you'll need a website to make sales, capture email addresses and present yourself as an authority in the field.

Step #5: Driving Traffic to Your Site

Now that you have this brilliant product or service, you'll need to find ways to tell the world about it. Getting people to visit your site will be your next challenge. You'll learn how to do that both on and offline, using both paid and unpaid means.

Step #6: Converting Your Visitors to Buyers and Opt-ins

Once you get people to visit your site, you'll want to get them to pull out their credit cards and give you money. If they don't buy, you'll want to get them to opt-in (to your list) to receive additional information from you, to hopefully sell them something later.

Step #7: Getting Your Buyers to Buy MORE and more OFTEN from You

Once you've convinced someone to buy from you, your next step is to get them to buy more. AND buy more often. You'll learn specific techniques to make that happen.

Conclusion

This book is all about a "system." A system I've created to help you succeed in the information product business. Follow these steps, in order and your chances for success will be much, much greater. Now, let's get started!

Chapter 5
Selecting Your Niche

Introduction

Deciding what kind of information you'll be selling is crucial to your success. You'll want to produce info products that are not just profitable, but on topics that hold your interest. Why? Because if you approach this business strictly as a money-making venture, you'll quickly get bored. If you do, your chances for success will be virtually nil.

Pick a niche where you can both make money AND have fun, and your chances for success will be significantly higher. Remember, niche selection is both an art and a science. You'll need to look at your numbers (more about that below), but you'll also need to "feel" what works.

Whenever I'm doing a seminar or giving a speech I use a line that encapsulates what I'm trying to tell you here. Find the INTERSECTION of your PASSION and PROFIT to select an info product niche. It may take a little longer to do things this way, but it will be well worth it in the long run.

To get started, you'll want to have a BUNCH of potential choices on the table. Start out by creating a list of everything you do pretty well. Don't censor yourself as you brainstorm. Let the topics flow. No matter how mundane or seemingly insignificant, write them down. Then take a look at your list (which is bound to have some 'strange' entries). That's good! Keep them. Do not screen at this point.

Next, take a look at your list and ask yourself: Can I do this particular "thing" better than 90% of the people out there? If the answer is YES, that items stays, and you now have a list of all the potential areas where you can create information products.

Your next step is to find out whether or not people are looking for any of the things you do well.

What Does Google Say?
Using Their Keyword Tool

Let's talk now about the "numbers" I mentioned above. Google has a great tool you MUST use before launching an information products business. There are others you can use, such as WordTracker, which costs money, but the Google tool is more than sufficient.

Here's the link: http://adwords.google.com/select/Keyword ToolExternal (This link may change. If it doesn't work, google the term "Google External Keyword Tool".)

From this link, put in the keyword or words you think people would search for to find out more about the topic you've selected as your niche. If you were thinking of creating products for bodybuilding, for instance, put in that word. Start with the most general term for what you do first. Once you do that,

Google will present you with a list of words that are associated with, or related to, the word or words you entered.

HINT: Make sure you're "signed in" to Google when you do a search using this tool. If you have a gmail account, or any other free Google service, sign in with that. This will give you a more extensive list of keywords as you search.

You'll also see a list of numbers associated with each word or word string, including a "local" and a "global" search number. If you'll be selling your information product anywhere in the world, concentrate on the global number, which indicates the number of searches done worldwide **each month** for that term on Google. The more general the term, the larger the resulting numbers will be.

How many niches are you looking for? It depends. You want a niche that is big enough to make money, yet small enough that you have a reasonable number of competitors. In general this means you'll be looking for a niche where Google's results fall somewhere between a low of 10,000 and a high of 200,000. These figures aren't etched in stone, but are a good place to start. If there are only 349 searches for a term, the niche is too small. On the other hand, if there are 525,000 searches, you need to "small it down."

For instance, if you put in the term "bodybuilding", you'll get more than 200,000 searches. If you put in "female body-building," however, you'll get over 10,000 searches but less than 200,000. Now we're talking! This is the size of niche you're looking for.

Your next step is to do a standard Google search for your niche word or phrase. In this case we'll use "female bodybuild-ing". At this point you're most interested in the sites which come up in Google's "organic" listings. These are the sites Google has selected as being the most relevant to your search string, as opposed to sites which appear based on paid advertising. If you're not familiar with how this works, organic listings are those that appear in the center of your screen, while paid listings appear at the top or bottom, (generally in a shaded box of some kind) and along the right hand side of the search page.

Now visit the top 20 sites that come up when you Google your keywords. Look at all of them. What are they doing? Are they selling anything? If so, what? How different or similar are they to the products you're thinking of selling? This research is key to helping you make a good decision when selecting your niche.

Keep in mind, however, that you want some competition. It's a positive sign if there are products being sold that are similar to what you're thinking of producing. If there are no similar products being sold that generally indicates a lack of demand.

Many people think they will have a greater chance of success if they pick a niche that is as wide as possible. Not true. Being more specific increases your chance of success. If you attempt to sell to everyone, you'll end up selling to no one.

Don't Just Niche it, Micro-Niche it!

I've established that to sell info products you have to find a niche so you won't have to compete against a large number of competitors. Whenever I do a seminar I use the following example to help illustrate this point.

To become really successful in any field, you have to become the KING or QUEEN of your niche. This means when people mention a field, YOUR name has got to be the first one that pops into their heads.

If I were to say the words "PERSONAL POWER," whose name would you think of first? If it's not Anthony Robbins, I'll be surprised. He "owns" this space. If I were to say GOLFER, whose name comes to mind first? Over 90% of people would say "Tiger Woods". Your goal is to eventually get to the point where YOUR name is top of mind when someone mentions a category. To make this easier you may have to "tighten" your niche, which is what we've done in the example above (female bodybuilding vs. bodybuilding).

With this book, I hope to solidify my position for the term: INFORMATION MARKETING. Although I'm fairly well-known in the field, I don't "own" the category. It's a tough space to compete in because there are a lot of people who claim to know the topic. My goal is to be the first name that comes off the tips of people's tongues when they say those two words.

Luckily, as of this writing, if you google the term: "information marketing", my blog comes out at #1!

I discuss many ways of getting to this point in this book, including writing the book in the field and having the blog. This section is about understanding the need to make your niche small enough that you can, in relatively short order, claim the title of King or Queen of your particular niche. (You can also think of it as a micro-niche.)

There are some obvious ways to micro-niche your topic. One is by geography, another is gender, and another is ethnicity. To give you an example of all of these in one place, I'll tell you a story about a woman who came to one of my bootcamps. She was thinking of putting together a product on how to invest in real estate.

I told her I thought the field was much too big and she should "small it down". We started by considering how to make her the "queen" of female real estate investors. Still too broad. We then moved on to making her the queen of African American Female Real Estate Investors. Still a bit too broad. We finally settled on trying to make her the queen of African American Female Real Estate Investors in the state of Oklahoma. Now she could target a small enough group to own the market, yet still large enough to make a good income.

Dead Center Keyword

Once you've done your Google research, you'll want to figure out what your DEAD CENTER keyword is for the niche you've selected. Picture this like the bulls eye on a dart board. There may be other words that get close, but there is usually one word or words that target your niche *precisely*. In my case, the words are "INFORMATION MARKETING", and everything I do is geared and directed at these dead center keywords.

As you start working on your business, always remind yourself of your dead center keyword(s). EVERY action you take should support your goal of becoming the individual or business who owns those keywords.

Number of Buying Units

Now let's take a look at the difference between the total number of units and the total number of buying units. In the self-storage industry, for example, there are over 33,000 facilities in the United States, however there are only about 21,000 buying units. Why the discrepancy? Because some people own more than one!

Let's take another example. I have a client who's trying to market products to the "rent-to-own" niche. Similar to self-storage, one person might own four of those rent-to-own locations; therefore, all **four** of those locations would be considered just **one** buying unit.

Chances are if someone owns four of these storage unit facilities, they are not going to buy four sets of materials. They're going to buy one unit and copy them for their other locations. (Even though they're not allowed to do this because of copyright laws, you should assume it's what they're going to do anyway.)

If they were a very large organization, however, (there is one self-storage facility that owns over 1,200 units) they wouldn't risk making copies because getting caught would open them to the potential of getting slapped with a huge copyright infringement lawsuit. (This is where you would have the opportunity to LICENSE them a set of materials.) What's important to understand here is that the number of buying units is potentially very different from the total number of units.

You've taken a look at the total number of buying units in your niche. Now you also need to look at their ability to pay. Do the folks you're targeting have a strong ability to pay, and a desire to pay, and a willingness to pay for whatever products you're going to create?

Some people will assess this opportunity inaccurately. For example, there is a well-known person in the self-publishing field who once told me "people like authors and publishers won't spend big money to attend an event". I've proven him wrong, repeatedly. Don't base your decision on what you think; base it on tests and results. Find out whether or not your market can tolerate and support the prices and the services that you are planning to sell.

What Direction is Your Niche Trending?

The next thing you need to do is determine whether the niche you are considering has an upward or downward trend line associated with it. It this niche shrinking or expanding? In the next three to five years do you see more or less people coming into this niche? If it's not an expanding niche, be careful!

Additionally, you'll have to ask yourself whether this niche has a decent turnover rate. Are new people coming into the niche? This is different from the direction the niche is headed. How much new blood is coming into the niche? The more, the better. Why? Because then more people can buy what you have to sell!

Can you find the folks that you're going after quickly and easily? Do they have a regular publication? Can you rent their names from a list broker? The easier it is to find and get to these people, the better the niche will be.

Where are the folks in this niche located geographically? Does it matter to you that many of them are outside the United States? Does is matter to you that half of them are in Alaska? Consider the physical location of the niche because when you start doing consulting work or seminars and training, you'll be traveling to these locations!

Now, didn't I just break my own "rule" by pursuing a niche like self-storage that only has 20k+ buying units? Yes. Rules are sometimes made to be broken. Self-storage operators happen to be a niche that are VERY willing to spend money on these kinds of products so I bent my own rules and targeted them. Good thing. It's become a VERY profitable niche for me.

You can take a mass-market topic, however, and niche it. For example, let's say you wanted to create a book on sales, which is definitely a mass market topic. In that case, you might consider sales for engineers, for example, "How to sell as an engineer." By doing this, you have taken your topic and found a "natural" niche for it.

There's one gentleman I'm coaching right now who's doing a product that's very motivational. His background is in high tech, so he's specifically targeting the high tech field. He took a mass-market message (motivation) and targeted it to a specific niche: high-tech. Even if your goal is to sell to the mass market, I suggest you pick a specific niche or two first.

Do not rule out anything you are interested in. I'm never surprised by niche market possibilities! Did you know that there are 250,000 rabbit breeders in the country? There are four trade publications for the rabbit breeding industry. And how about vintage pens? There's a huge resurgence of interest in vintage pens. Surprising? Hardly!

There's nothing wrong with doing something similar. Just make sure you don't copy someone else's content and ALWAYS give credit where credit is due.

It may take some time, but you'll find your niche. You just need to go after it – now!

Conclusion

Finding a good niche doesn't mean your success will be automatic. Approach the process like a baseball player approaches his season. If you can bat .300, you're doing quite well. If 3 out of 10 niches you get involved with are profitable, you're doing a pretty darned good job. Few people get it right the first time, which is why MOST people end up quitting this business. Don't be one of them!

Chapter 6
Writing the Copy to Sell Your Products/Services

Introduction

Copy is critical to your success as an information marketer. For this discussion, the term "copy" refers to the written words on your website, or the words in your videos, that are there to entice people to take action. This could be to buy your product (preferable), or opt-in to your list (usually your fallback position, but very important none-the-less.)

Why Write the Copy BEFORE the Product is Created?

Why talk about writing the copy before you've created the product? Good question. To create a great product you first need to create a great outline. How better to do this than by writing the copy that will sell your product?

Understanding that copy is key, there are two options: do it yourself, or have someone do it for you. My suggestion is that you always try do it yourself first.

There are two books I recommend you read before trying to write a word of copy on your own. First is "The Copywriter's Handbook" by Bob Bly, my favorite book on the topic. The other is Jeffrey Lant's "Cash Copy". An oldie but a goodie!

Writing the Copy Yourself

When you attempt to write the copy yourself, you'll find that it either comes easy to you or, more likely, it feels like a lot of work. When you're first getting started, I encourage you to do it yourself regardless of how difficult you find it. Writing the copy will help you understand how much work it is, and the true value of a good copywriter. And who knows, you may also discover you're good at it.

Also, if you don't have a lot of start-up capital, you won't have a choice. Good copy can be expensive!

Copy is critical because it can create huge differences in response rates. I've seen copy that, when re-written, closes as much as 900% better than the original. These results can turn a site that is highly unprofitable into one that's highly profitable.

This begs the question: how do you know what your results are? How do you measure them? Luckily, we have Google Analytics, which we looked at in the chapter on Systems.

Don't bog yourself down trying to learn all of the technical tools you need to use on your site. Remember, you are the subject matter/content expert, not the technical expert!

Since this is not a book about copywriting, this will be a very short chapter.

I don't want to get into the mechanics of copywriting here. I do, however, want to give you some important pointers to use when doing it yourself, or hiring someone else to do it.

First, start reading a lot of copy. This will get you familiar with how it looks and sounds. Next, take a look at FredInfoBoot camp.com. This site has a very high average visitor value. Use it as a model for what you do.

Copywriting is NOT my strong suit. I can write decent copy, but I always have it tweaked after I'm done. That being said, I have a template I use when I write copy for any product or service I sell. This template is courtesy of a copywriter friend of mine. Here it is. Make sure your copy includes all of these elements.

Your Copywriting Template

Start with a blank document with the following elements on the page. Then go through and make sure to include every element listed here.

Pre-Head
Headline
Post Head
Salutation
Opening Paragraph
Bullet Points
Testimonials
Offer
Price
Bonuses
Salutation
PS

Pre-Head

The pre-head is at the very top of the page (even before the headline). It is generally used to identify who the site is trying to target. For a recent seminar I used the pre-head: "Attention authors and publishers who want to dramatically increase income . . . "

This is the first line of copy anyone sees. If you have a banner on your site, it will be right under your banner. A change in headlines can often have a massive impact on your response rates. It's the single most important item in your copy.

Headline

This is arguably the most important element of your copy. Changing a headline can result in a 500% or greater increase in sales. The headline combines your biggest benefit with your customer's greatest need.

Posthead

Elaborates on what the headline says, or the promises or benefits made in the headline. Its purpose is also to get the reader to continue reading.

Salutation

How do you want to address the people you are talking to? What will you "call" them? It should be as specific as possible. Dear Friend is fine, but Dear Used Car Buyer is much better. Often the salutation is left out altogether. This is done when a traditional sales letter approach doesn't work. Again, this is an element you can test.

Opening Paragraph

Your opening paragraph's ultimate purpose is to get the reader's attention. Tell them why spending the next 5 - 10 minutes reading your content is worth their time. You need to emotionally connect with them and get their interest. Let them know you'll deliver on your promises. Do not bore them. If you do, you're dead.

Bullet Points

Bullet points are where you lay out the content and substance of the info product that you're trying to sell. You want to make sure and list the items in benefit (not feature) format. Many people will buy your product to get just ONE item in your bullet point list. To see how the pros do this, take a look at the *National Enquirer*, or one of the popular entertainment magazines in the supermarket check-out line.

Testimonials

Testimonials let your customers do the "selling" for you, and can be in a variety of forms. Written testimonials are good, but audio testimonials are better. Video is the best way to do them. Make sure when you record them you ask the right questions to elicit the best responses. The more specific you can get your customers to be, the more believable the testimonial will be.

Offer

What's your deal? What exactly are you going to give people for the price you're asking them to pay? This is the essence of your offer. An example might be: 4 1/2 hours of downloadable MP3 audios, a 120-page workbook in PDF form and a -minute telephone consultation.

Price

How much are you charging? Make it clear to people exactly how much your product or service costs. If you make it difficult or confusing to understand, they will make a decision to do nothing. Not good!

Bonuses

What will you give me in addition to what's in your offer if I buy now? Bonuses are critical to the success of your offer. Some people buy the product that you're offering just to get one of your bonuses.

PS

The PS is very important. When a reader reads your copy, chances are they will scan it, taking note of the beginning and the end of the document. That's why your headline and PS are crucial. A good PS will re-state the main benefits of your offer in a concise and easy-to-understand format. For example, "Remember, if you act by December 31st, you'll receive an extra 15% off the cost of (the product or service) and get a free (whatever) as well."

Of all of the copywriting elements I've listed here, you'll find the greatest improvements can be made by working on just a handful of these items. Concentrate on your headline and PS to start. Then consider testing your price and the bonuses.

Hiring Others to Write Copy for You

When you hire others to write your copy, you have two basic choices. You can either hire them to write it from scratch, or, you can have them tweak the copy you've already written. If you follow my advice, you'll want to write it yourself (most of the time) and then have someone tweak it for you.

Doing this will accomplish two things. First, it will help you to learn to write copy at a decent quality level. Second, it will save you a lot of money. The more copy you write, the better you'll get at it, but I still suggest you find someone who can tweak your copy to improve it even more.

For a flat fee a copywriter will take the copy you've written and make some basic changes to improve results. If you're not a professional copywriter, you'll find this service invaluable. And, if you're using Google Analytics on your site, you can see if it makes a difference, and if so, how much.

How much can you expect to pay? Copywriters who are willing to tweak your copy will usually do it for less than $1,000. That's a great value if it improves your closing rates!

Is it possible to hire someone from scratch to write your copy? Absolutely. Will it cost you a lot of money? Yes indeed, if you want someone good. Some of the very top copywriters, like my friend Bob Bly, will do it for somewhere around $15,000. WOW!

That's why I don't recommend you go that route, at least not when you're starting out. Additionally, it doesn't help you learn the basics of writing your own copy.

Copy for Audio and Video

If you choose to add audio and video to your site, you'll need to write the copy for both of these items as well.

Can you ignore my advice on this topic? Sure! But remember, I TOLD YOU SO!

Conclusion

Copy is critical to your success. You need to learn how to write it yourself. Whether you end up writing your copy in the future will depend on how good you are. After you get your business up and running, you may decide to use someone else to help you. If money is an issue, you will save a lot of it my having someone tweak your copy, rather than writing it from scratch.

Chapter 7
Creating Your Products

Introduction

Here comes the "fun" part - the actual production of your info product. In each section of this chapter I'll give you specific information about how to produce each individual type of product.

As you go through the material, please remember this key point. You do not need to buy the most expensive equipment to produce great products and make a lot of money. What you do need is **great content**. Keep that in mind when you create your products, no matter what "type" they might be.

People learn differently. Some learn by reading, others by listening, others still by watching and still others through an experiential event. Any time I do a speech or seminar I ask people to vote for which of those modalities would be their preferred primary means of learning. In every group I see the same thing. There are always a percentage of people who vote for each category. This distribution in a large group is often fairly even among the four.

What does this mean for you as an information marketer? It means you need to produce products using all four modalities of learning. If you don't, you'll alienate a percentage of your audience who prefer to learn in a way that you ignored. Bottom line? They won't buy your info products unless they match their style of learning.

In addition to producing products using different modalities, you'll also want to produce products at different price points. As an information marketer, you'll want to "lure" people to you with lower priced products, then upsell them to the more expensive products later, once you've gained their trust. The free material you make available has got to be very good. I call this the "Funnel System".

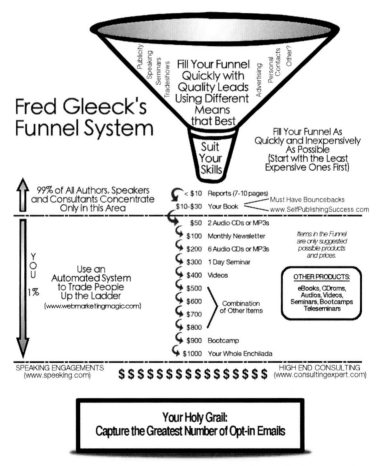

The funnel system is my model for selling information products. First, you need to create a skeletal line (initially) of information products. Second, you have to fill the funnel with quality leads at the lowest possible cost. Then you have to get those people to buy something from you – usually a relatively low cost product. Finally, you have to sequentially (and automatically-using autoresponders) trade customers up to higher and higher priced products and services.

When people don't know who you are, your chance of selling them a high-priced product is relatively slim. The more often you have contact with people and the more personal that contact, the better your chances are of selling them more expensive items. After they buy the first product, your goal is to "trade them up" to more and more expensive products and services. In a nutshell, you need to produce products using different modalities of learning, and at different price points – ranging from a low of $10 to a high of $1,000, or even higher.

By the way, you don't necessarily have to have just one product at each price point. You may have different products at each level. You may also create products at a price between these price points. There is no firm rule about how to do this, other than you need to have a line of products going from very cheap to very expensive using all the modalities of learning.

Free Material

Don't skim this section! This is really important for your success.

Your funnel starts here. What you offer your prospects for free is one of the single most important elements of your success as an info product marketer. You may offer a free report, a white paper or an audio interview. Whatever it is, it is critical to your success.

Anything you give away must be digital. (PDF's for written material, MP3s for audio). This will also enable you to capture their names and facilitate filling subsequent orders."

Given that building a large email list is key to your long-term success, one way to do this is by offering people who visit your site something for free. Most information marketers pay very little attention to this step. Bad idea!

If you create some really good free material, your chances for success go way up. Why? Because when people visit your site, they may not be ready to buy. As a fallback position you try and entice them with something for free. They bite, and download whatever it is you offered them.

If what you give them for free is GREAT, the chances of making a sale go way up. A speaker I saw at a recent seminar who worked for a major online newsletter publisher said: "We give our best **stuff** away for free!"

I built my email list almost exclusively based on this one idea. I offered people five of my physical books for free (in ebook form). All they had to do was go to: FredGleeck.com/ebooks. Over an 18 month period I added something like 75,000 people to my list.

So think about what you can offer your prospects for free. Think about it carefully. Make sure your target market would have an interest in the topic. Create a compelling title for your free offer, then deliver **much more** than what people would expect to get free.

Do this one thing right and you'll have people buying something from you in the near future. The following are ideas for products you can create and sell at various different price points.

Reports (Under $10)

Reports are a great low priced product to offer. They will typically be priced at under $10. Reports will be delivered in PDF form to those who decide to buy them. They should also be a maximum of 7-10 pages in length.

How do you determine what to write your reports about? Your customers and prospects will tell you. You'll hear questions when you are speaking at events. You'll have others ask you questions via email. Take note, these are great ideas for potential reports you can author.

Another great way to get ideas for topics is to survey your list. They will come back with topics you may not even have thought about.

Before you produce a report for sale, make fairly certain the topic is one there would be a fairly decent level of interest in. I don't want you producing reports that only one or two people will buy.

These reports should be very specific. Cover a very narrow topic, but cover it in depth. How many reports should you make available for sale? It will depend on your market. Start out with five. See how they sell. If they sell well, start asking your customers for other topics and write reports on those topics as well.

Some information marketers offer hundreds of low priced reports. This may not be right for you, but the only way to know is to get started and see if people start buying them!

How do you produce these reports? You can get fancy and use all kinds of high-priced software, but all I do is write them in MS Word, and then save them as PDFs. Simple and easy to do. I suggest you do the same.

IF you decide you want to make your PDFs look more attractive, I suggest you go to Elance.com, Guru.com or even Fiverr.com. You'll find people there who will be happy to create a 4-color cover for your document and format the document itself to make it look "prettier."

Like other digital files, these reports (once completed) can be uploaded into WebMarketingMagic and then sold for whatever price you decide to set.

Physical Book ($10-$30)

Writing a physical book about your topic of expertise is critical to your long-term success. Very rarely does anyone get press coverage for creating an audio or video, but they so with a physical book. Solely for this purpose it is imperative you create a physical, "real" book.

If you want to learn more about writing and publishing your own book, pick up a copy of my book: *Publishing for Maximum Profit*. You can download a free copy at FredGleeck.com/ebooks. If you are seriously interested in creating a "real" book, you need to get a copy! I won't give you more information here, because the topic is so huge. My book will give you everything you need to know.

Remember to speak with my friend, Ron Pramschufer, at SelfPublishing.com when you've finished writing your book. That's the best place to start. Tell him I sent you.

E-book ($10 - $50)

Your ebook can be simply your physical book in ebook form. The easiest way I've found to do this is to take the same files I use when I send my book to a printer and upload them into WebMarketingMagic. They would be in PDF form. If I want to sell the ebook for more money, I add some additional digital bonuses. Often times when I do this, I end up getting more for the ebook than the physical book.

Do you need any fancy software to do an ebook? Not really. I've seen many people write their book in MS Word and then save it as a PDF. People who will buy your ebook are mainly interested in content. They don't really care about a fancy color cover.

Creating Your Audio Products

Introduction

If you're on a limited budget, you can get started producing your audio programs for no out of pocket cost. Use your existing computer and the built-in microphone in your computer.

If you're doing an interview, it's also possible to use a place like FreeTeleseminars.com to record your interviews via a phone line. Skype also allows you to record your conversations for a very small additional fee, but I've found their service to be somewhat unreliable so beware.

Do-it-Yourself in a Studio

You can sit in a studio or in your living room and record an audio program "solo." You create an outline and just start speaking into a microphone. But no matter who you are or how engaging your voice is, this will *not* work well. Here's why. Even the best professional speaker gets boring to listen to (by themselves) for an extended period of time. It may work for a very short audio recording, but for a program of any length (over a few minutes), I do **not** recommend it.

Interview Format

A great way to produce audio products is to use the interview method, where you get a good interviewer to ask the "expert questions" and you record the give and take. Make sure if you do this that you choose someone who knows how to act as the interviewer.

Very few people can interview effectively. I have a product that addresses this issue specifically. You can find it at: Expert Interviewer.com. If you're planning on interviewing experts yourself, or even if you are the person being interviewed, you'll find this program particularly useful.

As is true with the creation of any product, a good outline is your key to success. Without a good, detailed outline, your chances for producing a good audio interview are much reduced. And without a great interviewer, your chances for success are zero!

Record a Live Event

One of the best things about recording a live event is the energy you can capture. When you do it right, live event recordings can be a great way to create your audio products. There are two keys to making them work well.

First, make sure the audience is properly miked. This means you want to have microphones in the audience that people can walk up to, or you can have mike "runners", and have the mikes brought to the person who asks the question.

As a listener to many audio products myself, there is nothing worse than having to try to figure out what an audience member is saying. Frequently, people start speaking without a mike. At my events I'm pretty militant about making sure people have mikes in their hands before they start asking a question.

Another tip to remember is to repeat questions from the audience, even if they are well-miked. It's a great habit to get into and people who buy your audio programs will love you for it.

It may sound like a bit of overkill to do both, but trust me, buyers will be delighted.

Creating Your Own Studio

You can create your own mini-studio in your home. The key is to understand the best quality recordings are produced in an environment where you keep the "bounce" to a minimum. To do this on the cheap just hang blankets on your walls. If you have bookshelves, slip the blankets under some of your heavier books to keep them in place. Also, make sure you have carpet on the floor. Doing this will deaden the sound waves, and make for a better sounding recording.

Have some extra money to spend? If so, you can purchase a self-contained mini-studio from a place called WhisperRoom.com. They come in a variety of sizes and are perfect for creating a soundproof environment. Be careful if you live in a warm climate as you'll need to make arrangements for cooling them in the summer.

Audio Equipment You'll Need

At the lowest end of the spectrum, all you need is your computer and a free piece of recording software. (Google this as these providers change frequently.) Using your computer's built in microphone you can record a decent sounding program without purchasing any additional equipment.

If you want to improve your sound from that point, invest in a decent microphone. You don't need to spend a lot of money and you can get some pretty good results. I own a pair of Fender P51 hand-held mikes that work really well. Last I checked, they were selling a kit for around $60.

I don't record onto my computer. Instead I use a Marantz PMD 660. I also have a PMD 670 to record my seminars and events. Both of these record onto compact flash cards and the sound is excellent. You'll end up spending around $500 for the PMD 660, but it's well worth it if you have the cash.

Recording onto Compact Flash is great. Once complete, it's easy to take your finished product anywhere. All you need is a very basic card reader that attaches to your computer. Depending on the size of the Flash card you get, you can record hours of audio material onto one card.

Software to Create Audio Products

I have never used a PC in my life. I only use Mac and Mac software. If you're a PC person, that's fine. But, I honestly think this business is tailor-made for the tools that Apple provides.

If you are using your computer to record and edit, Garage-Band is a great program that is easy to use and comes free with any MAC as part of the iLife suite of products. After you edit your program, you can then "send" the finished program to iTunes where you can create an MP3 version of the audio.

I also use my "Mobile Me" (soon to be ICloud) account to upload my audio files to a virtual hard drive. My webmaster pulls the files off of that drive and then prepares it for sale using WebMarketingMagic.

Once you use a Mac for your audio and video needs, you'll wonder how you ever did without them.

Audios: Physical or Downloadable?

Back in the "dark ages" I used to produce cassette tapes. Once completed they had to be physically mailed to those who ordered them. This was a nightmare! Producing and mailing them was a nightmare.

Every audio program I do now is not even available in physical form. For the older programs I still sell, I make the physical version available for sale, but for 300% more money. If people are willing to pay that much, I'll certainly ship it to them. If I offer the MP3 in downloadable form for $77, I'll charge around $297 for the physical CD. Again, still in MP3 form.

I suggest you follow my lead here. The freedom of having as much of your material as you possibly can in downloadable form is great. You can work from anywhere and don't have to worry about physically fulfilling any of your orders.

Producing Your Video Products

Your first question when thinking about doing a video is this: "Does it make sense to use video for this product?"

A number of years ago, I saw a video from a professional speaker. She had probably been told she needed to do a video, but didn't get it quite right. She was an expert on the topic of organization. When I played the video I saw her looking at the primary camera and speaking directly into that camera. Every few minutes she would then look at the second camera and continue speaking directly into the camera. Basically a "talking head."

If your topic is organization, video would be **perfect**, but not the way she did it. If you're going to do a video, bring your camera into my garage. Show the mess I currently have in there. Then give me some advice and show me how to make changes to make things better. Keep the camera rolling while you do it.

That's the right way to do a video.

Creating videos can be a bit difficult for those who have never done them before. The key thing to remember is that people are concerned much more with your content than with the quality of your production.

As a Mac guy, I use some very basic tools to create my videos. In many cases, I will not even do any editing. This is particularly true when I record a live event.

There are three basic steps to creating a video. First you have to shoot it. Then you have to edit it (if you're doing any editing). Lastly, you need to package it.

Video Equipment You'll Need

If you want to spend no money, you can use the built in video camera on your computer. My MacBook Pro can do pretty decent video with the basic camera that's built into the machine. If you do a lot of videos and want to move up a notch in terms of quality, all you have to do these days is get the new IPhone 4S.

I've seen videos doing side by side comparisons between the IPhone and a $3,000+ video camera. For me (and most mere mortals) the results were indistinguishable. After you shoot the video, you connect them to your USB port and import the video. It's virtually stupid proof! I need that.

I used to have some really high-end cameras, but I sold them all. I now shoot almost everything with my Canon Vixia HF200. At Costco they go for around $300 and they record video onto SD cards. I like not having tape, it makes things a lot easier.

As opposed to the Iphone, this camera also has a mike input. This allows you to get video that both looks and sounds good. Unless you're making super high end video, this is all the camera you'll need. Remember, it's all about content.

When I do a live event, I have four 16gb SD cards. This allows me to record around two hours of very high-quality video on each card. Most of the speakers at my events speak for less than two hours each. This way each speaker is on a separate SD card. Simple!

Seminars

In the seminar business, there is a "magic" formula. TR = SR + PS + CB. Total revenue (TR) is equal to seminar registration (SR), plus product sales (PS) plus coaching or consulting business (CB).

This topic is big enough that I've written an entire book about it. It's my best-selling book before this one. It's called

"Marketing and Promoting Your Own Seminars and Workshops". It's yet another one of the free books you can get at FredGleeck.com/ebooks.

If you like speaking in front of groups, doing your own seminars should be a product you consider. You may also want to try to get yourself a speaking slot at someone else's seminar on a topic that relates to yours.

Seminars are the only way you can get people to pay to be prospects. I have done close to 1500 seminars over the years. Not only can you make money from the registration fees, you can also make money from selling products and the coaching and consulting work you'll get. Seminars are an integral element of the product mix for any intelligent information marketer.

Speaking

If you love to speak in front of groups, speaking should be one of your info product offerings. Not only can you get paid to speak, but often your host will allow you to sell some of your other products and services. BINGO! Big money potential there.

You guessed it! One of my best-selling books is on the topic of Professional Speaking. It can be downloaded at the same place: FredGleeck.com/ebooks. If you want to learn how to "speak like a pro" you can also visit: TheSpeakingSchool.com. I hold that very exclusive event twice a year.

It's a lot of fun and you'll be amazed at how much you can improve your speaking skills in just four days. If speaking well is important to you, check this out now.

Bootcamps

Bootcamp is a word you'll hear a lot in the information products business. The word is used to mean a lot of different things. It almost always means an event that is three days or longer. When I use the term, I mean a long event that is very interactive and people leave with something they can actually use. Please remember that others may use the word differently than I do.

I suggest you consider doing a bootcamp as part of your info product funnel. For me, it's my highest price offering. The only other higher priced option is individual coaching and consulting work.

My bootcamps take place at my home. Do you have to do the same? Absolutely not. I like doing them in my home because that's my personality. I sincerely like people. At least most of them! If you enjoy spending extended periods of time with your "students" this may be the ticket for you.

To see what I do and how I promote my event, take a look at FredInfoBootcamp.com. Feel free to copy my model. It's working very well for me in my niche.

Software

A nice portion of my monthly revenue comes from Web MarketingMagic. It's the software I recommend every info marketer use to run their business. This is an indispensable tool in the marketing of info products. In fact, not only do I recommend you use it, I recommend that you get signed up as an affiliate to sell it. When you go the site, click on the button that says resellers at the bottom of the page. You'll receive 30% of the ongoing revenue from people you refer. Forever!

One of the reasons I've been able to sell a lot of this software is that it is a perfect fit for information marketers. They need it and when they use it they find it to be an indispensable tool. Many of my customers have been with me for more than five years.

I suggest you see if you can find something similar to sell to your niche market. If you can, you'll be in great shape. How do you figure out what people have to have? Ask them! As you get to know people you can ask them in person or survey them using a tool like SurveyMonkey.com.

There are two possible ways to go when selling software. Develop your own, or sell existing software. I suggest you avoid the temptation to create and develop your own software. Trust me, I've done it. It's a pain in the butt and you can lose a lot of money in the process.

As a big movie buff, I had a dream to create a community where others who were similarly inclined could get together and chat. I envisioned a huge number of people going to a site where they could talk with other movie buffs, read reviews and listen to interviews of people in the "business."

One day I was shopping for a mattress in Las Vegas. I went into a nearby mattress store and was approached by the manager. After talking about mattresses for a few minutes I said: "This isn't what you really do, is it?" He explained that selling mattresses paid the rent, but his real passion was theater. He went on to explain that he had developed the single most visited site on the internet related to Broadway and theater in general.

He gave me the name of the site. I went home and checked it out. I liked what he was doing but I was under impressed with the way he had pieced together various free software products to do all functions I wanted my site to be able to do.

So, I decided to create my own membership software. After spending close to $50,000, I realized I should NOT be in the software development business. I licked my wounds and went home. If you want to develop software, get some "pros" to do it!

If you want to develop "quick and easy" software programs, you should probably use a place like ScriptLance.com or Rent-A-Coder.com. These are sites where you can have people bid on your projects. I've gotten some pretty cool software developed for under $200. It all depends on how complex a concept you have in mind.

Coaching

Another "product" you can sell as an information marketer is your coaching services. Coaching is where you help people get what they want in a given topic area. I do a lot of coaching where I show people how to create and market their own information products.

I've written a book on my system for selling my coaching services. The title of the book is "Marketing Your Coaching Services." You can get it at the Amazon Kindle Store for just $2.99.

Coaching can be very lucrative, but it does require that you exchange time for dollars. I'm not suggesting you don't do it, but I would warn you to try and only do it on the "high end."

Here is my model for coaching, which I suggest you follow.

I offer people a one-time phone consultation for $100. In exchange for the money I'll coach them over the phone for 20 minutes. I let them use this option only once. If they want to continue to work with me, I have a separate model I use from that point on, and I have a specific website set up to allow people to take advantage of this option: ConsultWithFred.com. Take a look at it right now.

You'll see it is short, sweet and to the point. I detail all the terms and conditions. I suggest you set up something similar. That way, when people ask how your coaching program works you can direct them to a specific site and have the site do the "selling" for you.

As you can see from looking at the site, I allow people to apply the $100 towards other future products and services with me. I will give them dollar for dollar credit towards the purchase of any service priced at $1,000 or more. If someone pays me for a phone consultation today and next month wants to attend one of my bootcamps, I give them $100 off the bootcamp fee, because the bootcamp costs over $1000.

Many people will get everything they want from the phone consultation. Those who want more are encouraged to pay for and attend a FredInfoBootcamp. Take a look at FredIntoBoot camp.com for the particulars. This is a one week event where I work with up to six people at my house to get their info products business up and running.

In that week we spend together under the same roof we will both come to understand whether or not we could work well together in a longer term coaching arrangement. After spending seven days with people I can always tell if we would be a good match.

If we both want to continue I will then send them to The ProductGuru.com. This site explains the particulars of my long-term coaching arrangement. Take a look at that site now. I will no longer take on clients where there is no ongoing percentage. If I'm going to spend my time working with someone, I want it to pay off well long-term.

Another coaching relationship available to my customers can be seen at both FredProtege.com and JVwithFred.com. I suggest you again look at all of these sites and see how you can adapt and adopt what I'm doing to your business and niche. It beats reinventing the wheel.

If you are going to offer coaching, make sure you give people two options: one-on-one coaching and group coaching. To be honest, I often learn as much or more from my coaching sessions as those who are paying me for my help and advice. As Yakov Smirnoff used to say, "What a country!"

Consulting

Consulting work is one of the products you need to offer as well. It's at the high priced end of your funnel and is something that usually comes after you've developed some notoriety in your field. Don't' go after consulting work at the beginning. Like a number of the other items in your product funnel, I have an entire book written on this topic. Please download that book and get 200+ very specific and detailed pages of information on this topic. Again, you can find it at FredGleeck.com/ebooks.

Membership Sites

Membership sites are increasing in popularity. One of the reasons why is that some of the solutions are now very reasonably priced. In its simplest form, a membership site is where you take a website and protect various pages. This way, only people who have the passwords can get to specific pages on your site.

On the pages you protect you can have audio, video, text – whatever you want. The simple software now available just makes the specific pages you want unavailable to those who aren't members.

I don't care if you're incredibly non-technical, using a WordPress site and the software you'll find at CoolMembership Tool.com will get you up and running in a flash.

When do you want to set up and offer a membership site? When you have a lot of valuable content already developed and/or you create and crank out new content on a very regular basis. Some people are using the membership site software to make their material instantly accessible to people when they pay. This way they don't even have to download anything. They get a password, go to a page, enter their info and presto, the material they ordered is available to them.

I'm working on a paid membership site for information marketers now, but in the meantime, you can get a TON of great audio material for free at FredGleeck.com/training-videos. Go get it now!

The Importance of Your Product's Form

Many people who get into the information marketing business spend a lot of time worrying about the specific form their product should take. I've seen people who seem obsessed about whether a video should be in DVD, or streaming video, or downloadable form.

The answer: **deliver your product in whatever format your customer needs.** End of story.

The basic formats are written, audio, video, software and experiential. Virtually any form of product you can come up with will fall into one of these five general categories. As technology changes, there will be different methods of delivery, but the general form will not change.

Concentrate on creating great products. Anyone can use a delivery system. Only thoughtful, intelligent info product marketers can create great products.

Different Modalities of Learning – people learn differently, what makes sense?

Product Funnels.

The Problem with Products Looking Too Good

Making your product look too good can hurt you. Spending time on perfection at the expense of getting your product 'out there' so people can use and learn from it is a mistake. Content will always be king, so concentrate on that, not on how 'pretty' the product is.

Where Do You Get Your Material for Your Products?

If you are going to be an information product marketer, you'll need to be constantly creating new content. Where do you find new content? *Any and everywhere.* You need to be doing continual research both online and offline.

I do a lot of reading, both online and offline. As I'm reading, I always have my computer open and a text file ready to take notes. Don't ever think you'll be able to remember things. Write it down. Here are some places I suggest you look.

Google
Yahoo
New York Times
Wall Street Journal
USA Today
Books on topics of interest to you
Personal Interviews

Domain Names and Products

Whenever I get an idea for a new product, the first thing I do is reserve a domain name I would use to sell the product. I try and get the shortest, easiest to spell and easiest to remember domain name. From an SEO standpoint, it would be helpful to make sure the keywords are in the domain name itself. Reserve only .com domain names, nothing else.

The domain name is where it all starts. Before you invest a lot of time and money coming up with a product name, the .com extension of that name should be available. If someone else has the .com extension and you end up getting a lot of press and publicity, chances are you'll be helping them more than yourself.

I would of course recommend you buy your domains from UltraCheapDomains.com. This is my site and I get paid a small token amount for every domain you reserve. If you're going to be reserving a lot of domain names, it would make sense for you to go to SellDomainsForProfit.com.

This way you can set up your own "retail store" and sell yourself domains and make the commission. It only makes financial sense if you are reserving 50-60 domains a year. Take a look and see what makes the most sense for you and your situation.

Where to Buy Your Equipment

You can buy your equipment anywhere you like, just make sure you deal with a place that provides good service and good prices. Pay particular attention to their guarantee terms.

My personal choice for any and all equipment is a place called B&H Photo. It is based in New York City and their website is BHPhoto.com. They have extremely knowledgeable sales people, a wide selection, and a very good return and guarantee policy.

For a limited number of items I also use Costco (Costco.com) and Guitar Center (GuitarCenter.com). Costco has great prices and a great guarantee policy but virtually no sales help. Guitar Center has very knowledgeable sales people, good prices and a good return policy.

Once you figure out what equipment you need from B&H I suggest you see if that particular item is available at Costco. If it is, buy it from them. If not, buy it from B&H or Guitar Center.

Licensing

Licensing products can be a great idea. One of the best ways to get started selling info products is to find someone else's products you really like and sell them yourself. The most basic way to do this is as an affiliate. The term "open affiliate program" is where anyone is allowed to sell a product. All you have to do is sign up.

Other affiliate programs are closed. In these cases, you have to be approved to become an affiliate. There are various kinds of licenses, which I suggest you research. The basic ones are a resale license, standard license and master license.

In any and all of the cases, you can either BUY or SELL licenses. Some people may not offer the options I explain for you here, but you should know about them because you should be selling them!

In all of the examples that follow, I'll assume you're selling a $100 digitally deliverable product.

Resales Licenses

This is where you take your product and ask people to give you $300-$500 up front. After they pay that up front fee, they now have the right to buy your product and resell it at a higher rate of commission than the "standard" affiliate. Affiliates normally receive a 50% commission for selling info products.

If you have a product you want to sell a resale license for, charge anywhere from 3-5 times the retail price up-front and then give them an increased rate of commission between 15 and 25% points.

As an example, if a person paid me $400 to license a $100 digital product, I would then grant them a commission rate of 70%, instead of the standard 50% they would get as an affiliate. EVERY time they sell the product they would now receive the higher commission rate.

Standard License

I use the term "standard license" myself, but you may find others using a different name for this particular license.

In this scenario, the buyer gives me $1,000 (10-12 times the retail price) up front. They can then sell as many units as they like and keep ALL the profit.

The ONLY condition here and in ALL the licenses I sell is that the content cannot be changed in any manner, shape or form. So when a licensee sells the products he or she licensed from me, I continue to get all the bouncebacks that result.

Master License

This contains all the elements of the Standard License, but with an additional element. Anyone who buys a master license for a product of mine can then sell STANDARD licenses to whomever they choose and keep all the money.

In this case, I charge people 50-60 times the retail price for this option. With our $100 digital product example, this would mean between $5,000 and $6,000.

Again, they or any person they sell a license to cannot change the content of the program. All of the bounceback offers come to me.

If you have great products, licenses can be a HUGE additional source of revenue. Both from the money you receive from your licensees, but also from the bounceback income that results.

In all of these cases, you'll need a very good contract detailing your terms.

CONCLUSION

I know what you're thinking. There are a lot of products you have to produce. Don't try and do them all at once. Take a look at which ones makes sense for you to produce and get to work. Remember, they don't all have to be done overnight.

As an information marketer you'll be producing a lot of information products, but don't be intimidated. If you have an intense interest in your topic, producing these products will be more fun than work.

Make sure you start with a good outline and give your customers a product that gives them a very specific blueprint to take action. Make the products easy to use and understand. Give them more than they expected and they will always come back for more. Finally, remember that **done is better than perfect**. You can't make money with a product that is stuck in your head. Now, go forth and produce products!

Chapter 8

Designing Your Websites to Sell Your Products

Introduction

Your information marketing system should be online and web-based. The backbone of the system is the various websites you set up. As I said before, you have to decide if you will do this yourself or have someone else help you. Regardless of which route you choose, here are the essentials you need to know.

We've already discussed many of these items in Chapter 3 on Getting Your Systems In Place. This chapter will put things in the right order for you and add a few additional elements not covered in that section.

Let's assume you follow my advice and create a basic line of products. I'll assume for simplicity sake that you have created 10 different products. A few written products, a few audios, a few videos and a seminar or two. Each one of those products needs to have its own site to sell it.

In this scenario you'll end up with 12 total sites. First you'll have your authority site. This is where the bulk of your content will sit. You'll also have a squeeze page set up to capture names to fill your funnel. Then you'll have 10 separate sales letter sites, one for each of the 10 products.

This may sound like a lot, but trust me, it's not, and it's not expensive at all. Given that your hosting cost is fixed regardless of how many sites you have (assuming you're using CoolHosting Company.com), you'll be paying around $100 a year for the domain name fees in addition to your flat fee yearly for hosting.

Domain Name Selection/Registration

As I talked about earlier, the selection of a domain name is key for a number of reasons. First, you want a domain name that is easy to spell and remember. You also want the "best" domain name from an SEO perspective.

Take this part of the process seriously. Getting the right domain name will be very important to your long-term success. If you can't find an available name it may be worth it to buy an existing domain name. You'll find many good names not in use and available for sale.

Website Creation

Here you have two choices, you're either going DIY (do it yourself), or have someone do your website creation and design for you. Regardless of what you decide, make sure that you use WordPress as your platform. I also suggest you look at Cool WordPessTheme.com.

If you decide to do it yourself, pick up a copy of 7Minute MiniSites.com. This will make your life a lot easier. If you're like me and don't want to mess with the technical stuff, contact Dave Hamilton, the WebMarketingMagician at dave@wmmagician.com.

Hosting

If you have a domain name and you've designed a website, you'll need someone to host it. Go to CoolHostingTool.com for great prices and great service. This site gives you unlimited hosting for a flat fee, which is a very good idea if you're going to follow my system since you'll end up with a lot of websites.

Authority Site

Your Authority Site is one of the three main types of sites I recommend you create and use. I used to refer to this site as a brochure site. That name would probably work as well, but I think the term authority more accurately describes what you should be shooting for with this site.

For me, I use FredGleeck.com as my authority site. If your name is available as a .com, I would suggest you do the same. If it's not available, add the word "The" to your name. If Fred Gleeck.com was taken, I would have set up TheFredGleeck.com as my authority site.

There are two main purposes for this site. First is to get the attention of the search engines for your keywords. This will help drive traffic to the site. The other is to set yourself up as "the" expert in your particular niche.

You'll do this primarily by creating a huge volume of content related to the topic. You'll want to write a lot of articles, create audio programs and even do some videos if they make sense in your field. The authority site is also where you'll list all your accomplishments and show off your testimonials from happy customers.

In addition to FredGleeck.com, take a look at Seminar MarketingExpert.com as an example you can use to copy in your field of interest.

You'll also want to make sure there is a way to capture people's names when they visit your site. Even though it's not the primary mission of this particular site, you still want a way to get people to opt-in to your list.

Sales Letter Site

Sales letter sites are set up with the main purpose of selling you the product or service being promoted on that particular page. To look at my best example of this type of site, take a look at FredInfoBootcamp.

The way to evaluate the effectiveness of a sales letter site is based on the site's average visitor value. This site has a visitor value of close to $40 per visitor. This is extremely high and therefore worth using as a superior example of a sales letter site.

Squeeze Page Site

A squeeze page site has only one purpose, to capture email addresses. There are many ways to do this. Some sites use free audios or a free report as an enticement to get people to give you their email address.

Squeeze pages can take many different forms. Any squeeze page which maximizes the percentage of people who opt-in when they visit the site is a "good" squeeze page.

One of my JV partners, Bill Dewees has a very strong squeeze page that you can see at Voice-Over-Training.org. Take a look.

Membership Sites

There are a number of ways to create membership sites. Many of them are overpriced. If you are keen to set one up I suggest you start out using a very simple and inexpensive solution (WordPress).

For an example of what I'm talking about, take a look at the section of my site at FredGleeck.com/training-videos. Initially this was set up as a membership site. I've since opened it up for free.

It could just have easily been set up to make it so anyone has to pay to access the content. I've got a paid site in the works. You'll hear more about it if you're on my list.

WebMarketingMagic

WebMarketingMagic is an essential element of your website design. It must be included in any of the three types of sites you put up. You've probably seen me mention this site software FIFTY times in this book. Why? Because it's critical to your success as an information marketer. Make this the first thing you get. Here are the components.

Auto-Responders

Auto-responders allow you to set up responses in advance to send people an unlimited number of emails if they either buy or opt-in at one of your sites. This is a critical element of your success.

Affiliate Module

This module allows you to set up affiliates to sell your products and services. It's a very simple way to get yourself an "army" of straight commission sales people. There's no better way to get sales than to get others to sell for you.

Digital Delivery Module

People can download digital files for free or for a fee. You can set your system up to deliver any type of digital file (audio, video or text) for any price, including free. The system allows you to both sell and give away your digital material with this module.

Ezine Broadcast Module

Lets you stay in regular touch with customer/prospects. Once you have people who have either opted in to your list or bought any of your products, you'll have them in your database. This module allows you to communicate with them as often as you wish via email. Don't overdo it or they'll unsubscribe.

Auto-Responder System

Send as many automated messages as you want. As opposed to the module above where you can send out messages whenever you want, these are pre-programmed to go out. You can set up as few or as many emails as you want to go out to people either after they opt in or when they buy a particular product.

When you trade them UP to a different product, the system allows you to automatically unsubscribe them from one series of autoresponders and subscribe them to the next one.

Client Management System

Keep a database of your customers and prospects. Everyone who either buys or opts into your list will be on a "master" database that you can search. This makes tracking your customers super easy.

Coupon Module

Allows you to set up special "deals" using a coupon system. Want to offer a sale for the next 48 hours or until 100 units have been sold? This module allows you to do just that. It can create the urgency needed to get people to make a buying decision.

Tell-A-Friend

Makes it easy for others to refer people your way. There is nothing better than getting someone into your funnel by way of a referral. This module allows you to offer this option to people so they can share YOUR brilliance with others.

Automate Unsubscribe

Avoid SPAM complaints with this automated feature. Spam continues to be a huge problem for info marketers and can get you into a lot of trouble. Don't continue to email people when they no longer want to hear from you. This module automates the entire process so you're worry free.

Ad Trackers

Track the effectiveness of ads you place or links you suggest. Any and every link you send out can be tracked. This will give you data that is critical to your success marketing and selling information. This module will be invaluable for tracking your results.

Shopping Cart

Make it simple and easy for your customers to buy from you online. This is a no-brainer. Everyone must have a shopping cart. It allows people to buy from you online. This is a "standard" and necessary feature of any online system like this one.

Credit Cards

Give your customers a variety of payment options. Paypal is NOT good enough. If you only use Paypal as a way for people to buy your info products you cannot capture their names. Since your database is crucial to your long term success, don't leave this out of any package you get.

Conclusion

I've given you a lot to do here. Don't worry. There is no time frame attached to this project. The faster you get it done, the faster things will happen. But, the key is to get moving and get started doing SOMETHING. Do that now!

Chapter 9

Driving Traffic to Your Site

Introduction

Traffic is critically important to your success as an information marketer. There are so many sites out there competing for people's attention that you must find a way to generate a lot of highly quality traffic to your sites to succeed.

(Note: All the traffic in the world will do you no good if you can't convert your visitors. We'll talk about that in the next chapter, but please remember this fact as you go through this section.)

In this chapter, I'll give you a variety of different ways to generate traffic to your site. Don't try and do all of them. Pick the ones that give you the best bang for your buck and fit your skill sets and personality. I'll give you some very specific information about the top one or two elements in each category, and limited information about the others. Why? Because I want you to concentrate on the ones I highlight. They will give you the best return on your time and effort.

I've created four quadrants of traffic, which seem to make a lot of sense to me, and I think they will to everybody reading this as well. Here they are.

FREE – Online

SEO

SEO, or search engine optimization, is where I spent much of my time because, frankly, I didn't want to spend a lot of money. I started out years ago doing a lot of pay per click advertising and I got some decent results, but I really wasn't as diligent about monitoring my results as I should have been.

Search engine optimization is the method of doing things on your site, both onsite and offsite, that will get your particular site to rank as highly as possible in the search engines. (For the purpose of this discussion we'll use Google as our generic term for search engines.) Our goal with SEO is to get to the top of the 'organic' search listings. Organic listings are free, as opposed to pay-per-click listings, which are not. Organic listings appear in the middle of the page, while paid listings generally appear at the top, bottom, or right hand side of the page.

Content

When I go to Google and type in a few keywords, I generally stay on the first page of listings that come up, even if there are literally hundreds of pages I could scroll through. Occasionally, I'll go to the second page, but if your listing isn't on the first page, forget it, and usually, if it's not on the top 3 or 4, it's not really all that effective either. So when we're going for search engine optimization, we're trying to find a way to get us to the very top – within the top 3 to 5 listings – that's our goal.

Let's just boil it down to a few of the SEO basics here and we can elaborate on all these. Number one is that Google likes content.

You want to have a lot of really good written audio and video content on your site and you want to add to that content on a regular basis, over time.

You need to think about who your best users are going to be, or who your best visitors are going to be. One of the best ways to do this is to go into the Google external keyword search tool to try and find what we referred to as your dead center keyword. (Also pay attention to the other keywords that Google provides you that are similar to your dead center keyword. This will help you generate great, and targeted, content.

When you have great content, you will have a lot of people linking back to your site. They're called backlinks because when you go to a site and you really love it you say, "Hey folks, check out this site I saw." Backlinks are basically a sort of popularity contest with Google.

Google also ranks web pages based on the amount of time people spend on your site, often referred to as the "stickiness" of your site. This is one of the reasons I put audio programs on my site that are free to listen to, but you cannot download them. You have to stay on my site to hear them, therefore increasing my "stickiness", which Google loves and ranks highly. (It's also to showcase my expertise in this area, by the way, so it's a total win-win for me.)

Blogging

You should blog. I encourage you to use WordPress, and again, I would direct you to Dave Hamilton at AuthoritySites101.com. He can help you put up a really good-looking site, really quickly.

Here are some things to know about the blogging:

- Use a WordPress blog.

- Use tags in your posts so readers can easily find the blogs that pertain to their interests.

- Ask for guest blog posts. This will allow you to get good content without doing any of the work.

- Encourage people to sign up for your RSS update. If readers want instant updates when your new posts go up, encourage them to sign up for an RSS feed.

- Guest post on other's blogs. By doing this you draw a new crowd to your site.

- Comment on blogs, and leave links. When you can, comment on related blogs and leave your website address/blog address in the signature or web address field.

Every month about 500 unique visitors come to my SpeakingExpert.com site. Let's say that tomorrow I was interviewed in the Wall Street Journal about SpeakingExpert.com and I got a nice multi-column article written about us in the Wall Street Journal. What do you think that would do to the blog traffic?

You need to be ready for this sort of exposure because it can happen any time, and often when you least expect it. Imagine if you only had one blog post and suddenly a bunch of people went to your site. Not a good way to gain a positive reputation.

Your content needs to be fresh. If you don't have an intense interest in your topic area, I think your chances of being able to create a lot of content is very, very low. I always tell people, yes, it's great if you're doing your blog and making money, but if you're also not passionate enough about the topic to sustain your interest, you're going to lose steam.

Here's what I do to come up with new blog topics. First, I do a lot reading in my field. I have Google alerts set up which allow me to know when people say or do anything on line about various terms having to do with information marketing. The reason why I have that is, number one, I want to read what other people are doing, but I'm also intensely interested in knowing what's going on in my field so I can make various kinds of comments, particularly on my blog.

I post two types of content on my blog.

I post timeless content, which is something that will be relatively static.

I post timely content, which is content that changes with the day's news. With timely content I am looking for things that are discussed in my field. This requires more time, energy, and effort, but if you're intensely interested in the subject matter, it won't be that difficult.

Article Writing

Article writing is different from blogging in that usually you're going on these big, public article sites, like EzineArticles.com. Set up an account for yourself, and put together articles using your keywords and keyword phrases in the titles, and in the content of the articles. Then create a nice little bio section that leads to your site, and you'll not only get more traffic, but you'll begin to build your expert status in your field. (If you need help writing a bio, I suggest you check out www.writeagreatbio.com. Jill attended one of my bootcamps and I know she is really passionate about helping people write great bios.)

Can you submit your blog posts to article directories? I think you've got to be careful because if somebody starts to really research you and your work and see a tremendous amount of overlap, they might not be all that impressed. They might think you're just being lazy and printing up multiple copies of the same writing, or that you're using spinning software to create more keyword-based text.

Outside of that practice, I think anything you can do to get your name out there, in terms of your expertise and your content, is a good idea. So if someone agrees to let you write an article for them or put it on their site, I would do it gladly, as long as it targets the right group. If you're not writing for an audience who would be interested in what you have to say, you might be wasting your time – and their time too.

Linking Builds Traffic

Only try to get links from sites that are relevant in your field. Link exchanges were all in vogue for a long time, but I really don't think that it behooves you to just exchange links. What you're looking for are one-way links back to your site, anywhere you can do it. The link exchange is a way that people feel like they're both helping each other, and usually in a situation like that, one person is clearly getting helped more than the other.

Try to find big name sites where you can create some kind of a link back to your site – Yahoo!, Amazon, eBay, YouTube, etc.

But it's not just backlinks that count; it's also internal site links. Again, I am not the definitive expert on the topic of link building, nor am I an expert on the topic of link building within your site. Suffice it to say internal link building is very important because the more pointing you have to a particular page from other pages, including those pages within your own site, the more Google 'juice' is built up and the more Google will like you.

If your site is doing a pretty good job in the search engines, linking internally will only help to enhance that, so make sure, as you're building your own internal content, that you find ways to utilize internal links.

Forums

It's always good to have some interactivity happening on your site. It enhances your site's value and people stay longer. Forums also give people a reason to come back.

If you put a forum up, make sure that you participate as well. If somebody comes to your site and makes a comment on one of your blogs, and you don't get back to them for three months, there's really no incentive for them to keep coming back to see what's going on and to participate actively in the forum.

Video

In our MTV generation, people have really started to respond more to video than to straight copy. So what I encourage people to do is to understand that video is an essential element in their information marketing strategy.

Why? Because when someone comes to your site and sees a lot of copy, they may just pass right by it because they're short on time. If you have a video, the question then becomes: does the video try and get them to buy the product, or does it get them to read the rest of the copy?

I recommend a short video in which people get introduced to who you are, what your background is, what the product is that you're selling, and why it's so valuable. Most of these videos are going to run probably less than three minutes in length. If I go to a site and there's a really good compelling video, I will read all of the copy.

The short video performs the task of helping me understand whether or not I should even consider reading the rest of this copy, especially if there's a lot of it. The video isn't really to sell the product, it's to give you and your site enough credibility to convince visitors to read your copy.

Social Networks: Twitter, Facebook, and LinkedIn

I am not an expert in this field, but I have found it very helpful to use the basic bunch of social networks that seem to be in vogue these days – Twitter, Facebook, LinkedIn, and Google+. Everyone should set up these four accounts and try to develop a network of people who follow you. That way, when you have something of value to give away or to sell, you already have a waiting and interested audience.

Joint Venturing

Joint ventures represent the "one-plus-one equals three" concept… that you and I together can probably do more than you and I can on our own. The idea is that I'm co-opting some of your friends and colleagues who look at your work to look at some of mine.

JV partnerships vary depending on who's doing them. If you take a look at JVwithFred.com that's one example of a much more in-depth program that's very serious and long-term in scope. Other people do JV projects that are just one-offs. There's no one way it has to work. The whole idea of a JV partnership is just two people working together for some common goal, for a period of time, be it short or long.

Affiliate Programs

You can look for affiliate products to sell because it's going to be difficult for you to create a ton of products upfront. In the meantime, once you start developing your list in addition to your own products, you may want to sell other products related to your topic as an affiliate where you get a commission.

Usually that commission for information products is anywhere from 50% on up. If you're selling a product for $100 that someone else put together and you haven't yet created something like that, at least you can make $50 selling it with the 50% commission. It's a great way to earn income, and it's also a lot easier to promote other people's material than your own.

WebMarketingMagic has an affiliate program. This means if you wanted to set yourself up selling my products as an affiliate, you can sign-up for my affiliate program. You can put links on your site to get to some of my sites, to buy some of my products. And in exchange, you'd be given a commission based on your sales. This kind of an affiliate program approach is a really good one. Affiliates will get you a lot of traffic, especially if you have great products and you have sites that are good at closing people.

Reports and White Papers

A number of different people have done very, very well with the idea of reports and white papers for driving their website content. The goal is to write something really, really good that obviously relates to your field or topic, and that will make people say, "Man, this is great!" And they will hand it around and recommend and link to it, so a lot of people will see it. Bob Bly wrote a good book on white paper marketing, which you can find on Amazon.

Directories

There are directory listings that don't cost you any money. I would recommend you do it. It can't hurt.

Email Signature

At end of every email you send out, you may want to put something like, "To get six of Fred Gleeck's eBooks absolutely free, without even giving your email address, click on this link." I don't know how much traffic it is eventually going to generate you, but you should definitely be doing it.

Asking for Traffic

If people go to FredGleeck.com/training-videos, I literally tell people to please let other people know about this site. The only way to get traffic, and the only way to get anything in life, is to ask for it. Don't be shy, ask people to link and to share.

Podcasting

A lot of people go to iTunes and look at the popular podcasts in their field. Podcasting is something a lot of people have done very, very successfully. And if your podcast has the right keywords, or tags, and there are a lot of people looking for that topic, it can be a very effective way to get your word out there. People who download your podcasts on a regular basis are obviously the same people who are going to visit your site. Podcasts can take a little time to put together, but they are a great way to spread the word about your website.

Sharing Buttons

Stanley, my web guy, puts sharing buttons up everywhere on my site. At worst, they'll be ignored. At best, people will re-tweet, or post to Facebook.

FREE Offline

Generating press and publicity is usually the result of doing something the media will glom on to that is clever, different, unique, funny and crazy. The way you do this is by issuing press releases. Just remember, in order to get the coverage, you've got to do something unusual, different, and/or funny, so the news agencies find it newsworthy.

Public Speaking

Every time you get a chance to speak to a group, no matter if it is large or small, do it. You will get the chance to mention your website address, and over time this can be incredibly effective, especially if you end up speaking to larger groups of people.

Personal Contacts

A lot of people are too shy to promote what they do to other people in their personal network, yet these people can become your best connections. They will tell their friends, who will tell their friends, etc.

Referrals

People are also shy sometimes to ask for referrals, but this is a mistake. If you have a great product, program or service – whatever it is you're offering – ask people for referrals so your personal sphere can be expanded outside your own small group of people.

Working for Free

No matter what field you are in, there will be areas where you can volunteer your time, effort, and energies. One of the things people who volunteer always get is recognition, usually because they are not paying you. Recognition can come in various forms. They might put your website and website address in their newsletter, or you might be introduced at a public meeting.

Teaching

Any time you have a chance to teach a class for free, or even for a little bit of money, do it. It's great exposure.

Joining Associations

Joining certain associations, even though there might be a small fee, allows you to network with people in your field. However joining just to get a listing in the association directly will not be sufficient to drive a lot of traffic to your site. If you join and become active, on the other hand, you will get a lot more targeted traffic to your site.

Speaking at Someone Else's Event

If you can get booked to speak at somebody else's event, you're in a great position to do one-on-many marketing.

PAID - Online

PPC – Pay-Per-Click Advertising

One of the things that's nice about online paid advertising is pay-per-click (PPC) advertising. The top one we use is Google AdWords. The reason that PPC is nice is because it allows you to start testing your site almost within minutes of setting it up, and to get a quick sense of what you need to work on and tweak.

PPC ads work by sending people who click on your ads to various pages on your site. For sales, for instance, it's fairly obvious you will send people to your sales letter page and not your authority site. But if you have a really great authority site, that might be the best place to send people to generate opt-ins. (Almost as high as your squeeze page.)

Banner Advertising

Banner advertising was really popular in the late '90s and early 2000s. At that time they were pretty expensive, but after the dot com crash rates dropped dramatically, by like 80% or 90%, because they just weren't working.

A banner ad sits on somebody else's site, flashing, and trying to attract the attention of site visitors. I'm not against it as long as it's making money for you. Because of the drop in price over the past several years, banner advertising is now worth testing, If you have a banner on a good site, one that relates to your topic, area, or product, you might be able to make this work. For some people this works really, really well.

Normally banner advertising costs are measured in terms of cost per thousand impressions. (The number of times the banner appears on the site.) I recommend you try to pay around $50 for 2-3,000 impressions, which is enough to give you a pretty good idea of what your 'click through rate' (CTR) will be.

You may need to tweak your banner ad to improve your CTR, and you want to keep in mind that just a large CTR has nothing to do with dollars. If 30% of the people who see your ad click on it, but none of them buy, it doesn't matter. If 10% of people who click on your banner ad go to your site, and 10% of those people buy, now we're talking.

Advertisements in E-zines

Charlie Page has a publication called DirectoryofE-zines. com, which will give you a directory of all the e-zines and what they charge for their advertising. A properly placed ad in the right e-zine can be a really good investment.

In addition to ads in e-zines, solo mailers from companies that have relevant lists is another way to go.

Research is the key. If you were trying to target professional speakers and somebody had the most well-read e-zine in that field, it would probably be worth testing. The closer you can get to your particular target market, the better.

PAID Offline

Business cards

Your website address should be on your business card, and you might even put an offer on the card as well to compel people to visit your site.

Car Advertising

I used to run around with magnetic signs that I could just slap on my car, two on each side. I had a yellow sign with black lettering that had my website address and a tagline. That was actually pretty effective in driving traffic to my site in terms of the cost per dollar. Over the last couple years I've had my car wrapped, which means I put advertising wrap on the whole car, at a cost of $2000.

What I would have everybody listening to this program do is start out with a magnetic signs. If the magnetic signs work and work well, then I would consider wrapping the entire car, because we're looking at a difference between a couple hundred bucks max and a couple thousand dollars, a huge difference. Just be sure to include your website address and a tagline to make it easy to remember.

Join Your Alumni Association

Any association or alumni program that you have a legitimate right to belong to presents a great opportunity to network and/or be seen in a one-on-many situation. Do this if you can. (If it's not a great match, and it might not be, you can always resign your membership.)

Business Associations

The one offline business association that you should consider is your Chamber of Commerce, especially if you have a business that lends itself to that kind of networking. For very few dollars, you have the potential to drive some really good traffic to your site.

Trade Shows

Trade shows can generate interest, but paying for a booth can be pricey. I recommend you attend and hand out your business cards. Check out the trade show and see whether or not it generates business from this type of 'guerilla marketing'. You can get a booth at a later date if you decide it's worth it.

TV, Radio, or Infomercials

This is something you should know exists and consider, but generally this is not for someone who has a small budget. Although in some markets radio advertising might be effective, most of the time this requires a serious test to make sure you're not blowing your money on something that's not going to pull very well.

In these economic times, the radio and television areas are hurting for money because advertising is way down, so you may want to consider producing something for radio and television, and see if you can get in with even a small 30-second spot.

Writing a Book

A book is your single best promotional material piece, especially at live events.

Direct Mail

Direct physical mail's response rates have gone up, especially since everybody's doing email marketing now. When you're promoting a website, probably the best way to do this is with a postcard.

Misspelled Domain Names

A misspelled domain name will end up generating you traffic. For example, I own Speeking.com, and that redirects to a site on professional speaking. You may want to consider reserving some of the misspellings of your domain names.

Conclusion

Pick one or two items from each quadrant to really concentrate on to start. Pick those by defining your basic nature, what are you best at, combined with what is the most effective means and method of marketing to get traffic to your site. If you are not a really outgoing person, and do not enjoy speaking in front of large groups, don't choose that option! Choose what you're good at, and enjoy. The most important thing to do is *just do something!*

Chapter 10

Converting MORE Visitors into Buyers/Opt-ins

Introduction

There are two primary things you want people who visit your site to do. The first obviously is to get the visitor to buy something. Your secondary goal is to encourage people to opt-in. In the event that people don't buy, you should also have some tracking mechanisms that determine whether or not they opt-in to your list, which means they give you their email address for future contact.

You don't just want to increase the site traffic. You want to turn your visitors into buyers, and there are a number of ways you can do this without spending more money – or too much time on your site.

Primary Elements to Increase Conversion Rates

Videos on Your Site

It's starting to be shown that in most cases one of the most effective means of converting people, either to buy or opt-in, is with a video. Now again, we've talked a little bit about video and how to do it, but I would suggest that everyone have a video on their site. In the event you've got a face for radio, you may want to hire someone to do this. But again, you're trying to set up a relationship with your audience based on trust, honesty and understanding, so showing your face may not be a bad thing.

Keep this video relatively short, probably less than three minutes. And again, if your goal from that video is to establish yourself as a knowledgeable expert and get people to opt in, make sure you talk about your expertise and guide them to the opt in page.

Headline

Other than the video itself, whatever you put as the headline on your site is going to be most important in getting visitors to take the action, which is to opt in. Again, think carefully about this. Keep testing different headlines and get better and better.

(Note, you must have Google Analytics installed on all your sites if you are going to be testing anything.)

Bullet Points

People who are coming to your site for the first time are looking to get a quick picture of what it is you have for them, so bullet points are important. The major thing to remember with the bullet point is to make sure you don't have to scroll down to see them on the site. You want to have three or four powerful bullet points that are filled with benefits in and above the fold on your site.

Subhead

Usually your subhead appears directly beneath your headline. A subhead's function is to further describe what the headline is about. Look at your site and see whether or not you have the space, and whether or not conditions merit, using a subhead.

Video on Sites

If you're going to put a video at the top of your site, it must immediately engage the person who is watching the video, and convince them they are the right person for your site. So going back to the example of speakingexpert.com, a video aimed at them might start, "Hey, if you're a professional speaker, you've come to the right place, because a lot of you are suffering with the following situation: which is you're not making enough money; you're not getting as many gigs as you want. Isn't that true?"

In other words, you're going to talk to someone, hitting them immediately with some of the things, the components, that go in to a headline, which is: What is their biggest need? What is their biggest hurt? What is their biggest pain? And how are you going to be the one to alleviate that pain, hurt, or need?

Testimonials

Your testimonials should be as specific as possible in order to have maximum effect. Just saying something very glowing about you and your materials isn't nearly as important as saying something very specific about the particular thing you're trying to get them to do, which is again, either to buy or to opt in.

Pop Ups

If you go to my site, you'll find a pop-up that comes up immediately upon entering that takes you to my Fred Info Boot

Camp site. This is because one of my bigger goals is to get people who are reading my site to eventually attend the boot camp.

Annoying? Maybe, but the question isn't really whether or not they annoy you. The question is whether or not they get the results. And the answer to that, in most cases, is yes. Therefore we use them.

Fast Load Times

People will leave your site if they think it is taking too long to load. Don't forget to test yours.

Browser Compatibility

One of the things people often neglect to do is test their site in a variety of different browsers, which include Safari, Firefox, Chrome, and Internet Explorer. Some sites look different on different browsers. Check yours.

Easy to Read

Readability is impacted by your font choice and a lot of other factors – white space, color choices, etc. When you go to your site, make sure it is easy to read.

Dual Readership Path

In addition to the copy that you create for your site, you also want to make sure that you're using headlines and sub headlines within your copy. People should be able to scroll down and skim through your site by looking at these headings.

Y-O-U oriented

Often times I see copy that's very 'me' oriented. The site is all about them and what they've done etc., as opposed to writing for the site visitor. The more 'you' oriented or the more visitor oriented you make the site, the better it'll be in terms of conversion rates.

Focus on Benefits and Not Features

Newbies still think they should list everything their product or service will do in a laundry list of features. In fact, it's the benefits a customer will get as a result of using your product or service that's critically important.

Talk to a Specific Individual

People often write and create their sites generically, so they're talking to everyone. Remember when you're putting your site together, in terms of the copy, the video and everything else, that you are addressing a very, very specific individual person. This tip alone will help you really get your site converting better.

Pictures

In addition to video, make sure you have some pictures of you and/or your office somewhere on the site. This small addition will give people an idea of who you are, and that you are a real person.

Guarantees

Don't make guarantees so large and so big that they are unbelievable, but do put in some guarantees (even on free items) because even though the product might be free, that person's time isn't. Guarantee they will get certain results. Don't overdo it, but make sure a guarantee is somewhere on the site to help conversion rates.

Customer Support

The customer support issue is something that can be critical. By customer support, I mean just make sure you are doing what you would expect others to do with you if you went to their site.

Phone Number

I use my Google voicemail number and this allows me to set up an address. If you go to SeminarMarketingExpert.com, or any of my sites, the number you see is a Google number that allows me to screen calls if I want to.

Don't Hold Back

Customers need to know you're not holding back any vital or important information until after they take an action. Give people all the information up front, rather than saying to them, "…but if you get this then I'll give you something else". That hurts your credibility.

Lack of Action

Make sure you tell people what not opting in, or what not buying this product will do, and what they will miss out on.

Answer Questions Before Customers Ask

Think of all the questions that someone coming to your site who doesn't know who you are would ask. Use this information to write a Frequently Asked Questions page (FAQs).

Using Scarcity

Scarcity means that you have a certain limited number of units available for sale, or for opt-in, and is one of those things that can propel people to act. If you use scarcity just make sure you use it realistically, and that you actually follow through.

If you're offering something digital for free, the scarcity element might be that at any time you can discontinue the offer so visitors should "opt in now".

Study Your Competitors

Knowing your enemy is vital in helping to increase your conversion rates because the idea that people are not going to check out and spend time on competitive sites is foolhardy. Study what your competitors are doing and see if you can learn anything from them.

Do Not Use Flash

Some computers do not use Flash, so neither should your website.

Your First Page Should Be Your First Page

Make sure your site visitors don't have to click on the front page to get to your site. Once they arrive, they're there.

Have Multiple Versions of Your Product

If you are trying to get the people to buy something, it might be a wise idea to test different versions of your products, different price points, etc. When I say multiple versions of your product, I'm just saying remember that people may respond to different approaches, and therefore it might be wise to test both different price points as well as different versions or types of your products to see which converts better.

Explain How and Why You are Different

People are going to be visiting a lot of different sites related to your topic, so it's important that you make sure and tell them how and why you're different from the rest.

Use the Right Font

Use easy to read fonts that don't include a lot of swirls or flourishes. Older eyes can't read those fancy fonts, and they might just avoid your site completely if you use them.

Have a P.S.

A PS is one of the most highly read items in any letter, sales or personal. People generally start at the top and then scroll down to the bottom. The PS is like a second headline, so make sure you put a PS on any site you have.

More to Know

You have been given a laundry list of primary elements to test conversion and you should look through all those again to make sure you are using at least some of them. These are the secondary elements that should also be considered. Again, don't try and do everything at one time but understand that all of these are important.

Multiple Payment Options

Make it easy for people to give you money, by PayPal, credit card, check, or cash, whatever you can do. The more ways you make available for people to give you money, the better off you'll be and the more money you'll make.

Explain the Delivery Process

If people are buying a physical product or something that is delivered to them, or digital for that matter, they want to know how they are going to get it. To increase your conversion rates, let people know exactly how things are going to happen once they press submit or press buy.

Toll Free Phone Number

A toll-free number is a good idea even though most people are on cell plans and other plans where they have unlimited calling. The toll-free number is good because people don't perceive they are paying for the call, number one; and number two it adds credibility to you as a seller or provider of information. I encourage people to get a toll-free number. It looks better.

Site Counters

Don't have one. It's a bad idea.

Be Specific

Be very, very detailed and specific about the offer you are making or the product that you are selling or the opt-in item that you are offering.

Bonus Offers

Bonuses that are related to whatever it is you are offering are an excellent item to help increase conversion rates.

Build Value Before Giving Price

Don't give out the price of a product before you've first built a lot of value by explaining exactly what they'll get and what the benefits will be. Build justification first before giving out that number.

Use a "REAL" Address

A real address should be listed on your website to boost your credibility.

Website Colors

Make sure that your site is easy to read and pleasing to the eye. I find many sites out there to be really, really abysmal in terms of the color selection, and this turns me off.

Visitor Privacy

When people are opting in or buying something, make sure you have a privacy policy clearly stated on your site. If they give you their name and their e-mail address, the last thing they want to be doing is getting tons of spam from you.

Don't Beat Around the Bush

If you're trying to get them to opt-in, be very direct. Tell me what you want me to do and don't beat around the bush.

Call to Action

Let people know what it is they are there for, and what it is you want them to do. Don't make it difficult for them to understand what action you want them to take.

Increasing Visitor Site Time

We've talked about this before in other parts of this program, but getting people to spend time on your site is an essential ingredient of getting higher Google rankings. Have videos for them to watch, audio, etc.

Keep Your Site Simple

Don't go overly complex on your site, just keep it simple and tight. Simple helps conversion. Complex hurts it.

Be Different/Controversial

You want to be different, unusual, and possibly even controversial so people start talking about you, and they tell their friends, who tell their friends…

Make Videos and Audios Real

The more authentic and real your videos and audios are, the higher your conversion rates will be. The more people feel you're sort of faking it and putting on a persona for that particular item, the less effective it will be.

Having a Reason Why

Answering the question "Why?" is vital to writing good and effective copy. "Why" is telling people why you're giving this away, or why you are selling it and selling it so apparently cheap. Whenever you do something in which you ask people to do something, explain to them why.

Make Contact Information Clear

Have you ever been on a site and had a hard time finding contact details? Huge mistake! It's very important you have a way for people to reach you to ask additional questions, or for more information. Make it clear how that happens.

Only Ask for Relevant Data

In most cases, name and e-mail address should be sufficient to get people going. No more than that.

Show How Your Product Saves Time and Money

The two most important things to get people to convert to either buy or opt in are to show them how something you're going to give them will save them time or money.

Simple Site Navigation

Do not make a site that makes it difficult for me to get around, because the more you do that, the shorter my visit will be.

Study Your Competition

Yes, again.

Last Resort: Get an Email

The last resort means that when your site visitor starts to click away from the site without buying, you throw up a pop-up that says, "Wait, wait, wait! Before you go, here are some great digital bonuses that you can get for free if you just give me your e-mail address."

Amortize Your Pricing

Consider this if you have a product that is fairly pricey. Rather than say it's $1000, give them the option of making four payments of $250 each. That makes their buying decision much, much easier.

Keep Your Style Consistent

Make sure the site looks the same from top to bottom. That there is consistency in terms of how you present, whether it is fonts or colors or anything else.

Conclusion

Keep this checklist of items separate. The site that you put together will be constantly evolving and your goal is to increase the number of people who either buy or opt-in. You want to do that by making sure you are using all of these different techniques, but not trying to do them all at once.

Great results don't happen overnight. Great results are achieved by testing and tweaking your site over time. The worst your site will ever be is the first day you put it up. As you start testing and tweaking, your results will only improve. Get obsessive about testing. It will be one of the most important things you do as an information marketer.

Chapter 11
Getting Buyers to Buy MORE of Your Products

Introduction

Once you've gotten someone to buy from you, the "trick" is to get them to buy more AND buy more often. You're trying to get people to buy from you more frequently as well as increase the average size of their order. Let's talk about how to make that happen.

Getting People to Buy MORE

UpSells

An upsell is what McDonald's does when they say, "Do you want fries with that?" In other words, once someone has made the decision to buy, or has already bought, they are given the opportunity to add something else to their order.

A program like WebMarketingMagic has a number of these upsell components built into the system that can be easily implemented.

The key is not to upsell something that seems completely unrelated – that will hurt your sales. (Why am I being offered a fishing pole when I just bought a cake pan?") My feeling has always been that the suggested upsell is good to go at anywhere from the 20-30% range in additional pricing. So, if you're about to buy a $100 product, my offer to you should be somewhere between $20 and $30.

You're not looking for a huge additional sale, you're just trying to get a little bit more money out of the sale you've already made.

Additional Products – Like Amazon Suggests

Amazon does this well. "People who've bought this book also bought…" What do you have that you could be an additional product?

I think of this component as happening *before* they get to the actual order page, where they're already committed to ordering, and more likely to add on another item that would benefit them.

Bundles at Discounted Rates

Bundling is a good way to get people to buy more. If people are interested in a certain product line, be it a specific product or a service, you can bundle things in and make it more attractive. For example, I'm going to be selling a lot of licenses and I say to people, if you buy two to five licenses you get 10% off your total order.

If you buy five to 10 licenses, you get 20% off. And if you buy 10 or more… you get the idea. Bundle similar things together and give people a discount. That will also encourage them to buy more, which means they'll spend more dollars in that initial purchase.

Write Great Copy

I consider this to be upselling in advance. When offering a certain product, you might have a PS at the end and say, "Hey, by the way if you get this, this, and this it's a lot cheaper! Here's what they would normally cost…"

I might set up a separate page for the bundled offer. At the time they're ordering individual products, you may want to present them with that possibility.

Make Irresistible Offers

Generally, you only have one shot at people to make that initial sale so I would say making an irresistible offer is really crucial. Don't hold back and think later on you'll really give them something special. Think that you really only have one shot and make the best possible offer.

Getting Buyers to Buy More OFTEN

The more buyers buy, the more you make.

Deliver Great Products

We've talked about my ten times rule, which means if you produce something you're going to sell for a $100; you've got to give people the feeling they would have been willing to spend $1000 for it and still get good value from it.

If you deliver great products and people go, "Holy cow, this was unbelievably good," their chance of buying more often goes way up. It's important to deliver a great product; and by a great product I mean something that's easy to understand, easy to follow, gets results, and does all those things great products are supposed to do.

Build the Relationship with Them

This business is sort of like dating. You go out on the first date with someone and if it's a great date you want to go out with them again. In order to do that, you've got to build a relationship with them. You've got to show them that you not only care about their money but you care about them, and what their needs are, and giving them what they want. That relationship building is done with a few different tools.

Auto-Responders

The two primary things you are going to build relationships with are the tools you get in your WebMarketingMagic system, including auto responders. Auto responders are automated messages that go out whenever someone buys a product or a service, and they go out on a regular basis, maybe once every three to four days for a period of weeks or months.

Regular E-zine

Another element that is critically important is a regular communication with your customers that is totally unrelated to their buying of that product, but it is still in the field. So if I bought product A from you I would be getting a series of auto responder messages about that specific product. That's what I would call timeless information that you're giving out with regards to that product. The timely information is a regular E-zine, something they receive that is related to your field and is based on current events, not necessarily based on the product they bought.

You're trying to build a relationship with them hopefully to get them to buy more in the future. The last thing you want to do is continually pump them with sales messages. The messages you send to them, in both the auto responders as well as the E-zine, shouldn't be packed with sales. The person who gets them shouldn't say to themselves, "Oh no, not another sales pitch."

A good ratio is about three or four to one, which are four content messages to every sales message. For example, I send you an auto responder and 80 percent of it deals with great content. At the end I sort of pitch you about another product I have. That's fine.

People are willing to tolerate that. But if 100% of your auto responder is a sales message, I'm going to be resistant.

Within Your Products

Within the product they buy you're going to impress upon them the need for other additional products that should be bought as well. Your goal here is to get them to buy more often. Within the products themselves you're going to have a few little hidden and not-so-hidden sales messages for them to buy other products and services because certain things that you're covering in Product A will also be better and more enhanced if they buy Product B. So within Product A you're going to make subtle and sometimes not so subtle references to why they should buy product B.

For example, let's say you were going through my program. We've been talking a lot of the how-to's of information marketing and info products and how to create them and how to sell them. And during the course of this particular program we've talked a lot about other products I have like WebMarketing-Magic. Now although I've used that frequently I think it's been perfectly appropriate because it is something that you need.

The only problem people have is when they start to feel badgered by someone to buy something with no real reason other than it's going to help me make more money. The intent should be, "Because we're talking about hosting, one of the things you should use is CoolHostingTool.com. Well, CoolHosting Tool.com happens to be a program in which I get an affiliate commission. But there's nothing wrong with that because it was perfectly appropriate to bring it up.

I don't think it's a bad idea to suggest products as long as it really does make sense.

Show People How to Use Your Products

If you get someone to sign up for a health club, but they never go, what's going to end up happening when it comes time to renew? They're going to cancel.

There is a really important lesson here. Once you've gotten people to buy the product, you should also be trying to help them consume the product. Why? Because if they consume the product they'll be much more apt to buy another product from you, and also much more likely to see the various bounce backs and upsells that are inside that product if they actually go through it.

Continue to Prove You Are a Leader

In order to get people to buy more often they've got to see you doing things in your field that shows them you are someone they should follow. For example, I do weekly webinars in information marketing, and people can see that on my site if they go to FredGleeck.com/webinars.

They can sign up to participate in these webinars for free. So I have to constantly produce new products and attempt to be 'seen'. People should not look at you and see someone who produced one product 10 years ago and is now resting on their laurels. That isn't a way to get people to buy more often.

Again, this is why I suggest to people they **do not** approach information marketing in a mercenary fashion, because if you're really into a topic it's going to be a lot easier to stick with it and stick with it for the long run.

Good Follow-Up

Good follow-up occurs both in on-line and off-line methods. Your goal with follow up is to establish a relationship where the customers comes back and buys from you again, hopefully again and again. Therefore following up is crucial, online, offline, or both.

For example, I recently bought something from a well-known merchant. I got a call a few days later asking, "How was everything? Were you happy with this?" (Just remember when you do that kind of follow-up you have to be prepared for negative feedback as well.)

Continue NEW Product Creation

If you're in a field and you want to get people to buy more often you've got to have more things to buy. The process of information marketing should be an ongoing process where you're constantly creating new products. On average, I probably create five to ten hours' worth of usable material in some form every week. Some of it is free, some of it is paid, but the important thing is that I am continually producing information in the information marketing field.

At the same time, you've got to make sure you create great products at the fastest clip you can without disappointing the people who receive them.

Conclusion

There's a big difference between success and huge success. Use the tips in this chapter and you'll rise higher and faster than the crowd.

Chapter 12

Conclusion

Now that you're done reading this book, I have a few suggestions for you.

1. Read it again. No matter how much you think "you got it", the second or third time through helps you to more fully understand the concepts and ideas.

2. Follow my system. Rather than change the system I've given you, follow what I've suggested here. After you've done it a few times, then you can start "doing it your own way."

3. Get on my list at FredGleeck.com. This will keep you up-to-date with the latest information in the field.

4. Don't believe MOST people in this field, they tend to "embellish" their numbers and results. Only believe your own numbers. Don't be disappointed, results take time!

5. Become the best known person in your niche. Do that and everything will be easier.

6. Get started! Most people do nothing after they read a book. Take action! NOW!

7. Attend one of my events! Self serving? Yes!
   A good idea for you? Absolutely.

8. Buy some of my products. Again, do I benefit? Sure.
   But YOU will benefit more!

9. Don't quit. Most people who do this will. If you don't,
   you'll have a much greater chance of success.

10. Build Your own large list. Do that first and everything
    else will follow.

Recommended Reading

In addition to this book, I have some others books that I consider mandatory reading for any serious student of information marketing. Here is the list.

"Free" – Chris Anderson
"Talent is Overrated" – Geoffrey Colvin
"Outliers" – Malcolm Gladwell
"The Dip" – Seth Godin

Fred Info Bootcamp

If you've enjoyed this book, I suggest you now consider attending one of my one week-long events in Las Vegas. In 7 days I'll walk you through the entire 7-step system. You'll leave with an audio program recorded, a website up and a complete understanding of the process.

Why spend the money? Why not just do it yourself? If you can, then by all means do so. I suggest attending the bootcamp if you're like me and need a "kick in the butt" to get things going.

Frequently when people attend one of my seminars (of any length) they leave knowing what to do and how to do it but they *don't do it!* Why not? Most of the time, life gets in the way. I've found that when people set aside a week of time to do this and nothing else, it gets done.

To find out more about this event, make sure to visit FredInfo Bootcamp.com

Book Updates

As I said at the beginning of this book, things change very quickly in this field. To keep up with those changes, please visit: SellYourBrainPower.com. You will be able to find the latest and most up-to-date material in the field of information marketing.

NOW . . . . GET GOING!!

Resources

Here are some of the resources you'll need to help you succeed as an information marketer. I only wish someone had given me a list like this when I first started. It would have made my life a lot easier. I encourage you to visit all of the sites and resources I recommend.

My Sites You Should Visit

WebMarketingMagic.com

Need a system to run virtually every element of your business in the information marketing business? This site will give you the tools that you need to run a successful info products business.

UltraCheapDomains.com

Want to register domains for the lowest prices around? This site will show you how to get the lowest prices around to pick up or renew a domain name.

FredInfoBootcamp.com

If you want to learn how to create, market and sell your own information products, this is THE site to visit. You'll see how you can build your own information marketing "empire" in a week's time.

FredGleeck.com/blog

If you want to hear the latest ideas and "buzz" in the information products business, this is the site to visit . . . every day!

ConsultWithFred.com

Want to learn how to get some individual help on your project? This site will show you how to get a reduced rate for one-on-one help. This is relevant regardless of the field you're in.

LunchWithFred.com

Get together with me for lunch when I'm traveling. Up to 8 people can sit at lunch and ask me any question they want about any topic. Go to the site to see what city I'll be in next. It's always fun to get to know you personally.

JVwithFred.com

Want to get some personal mentoring in the information marketing business? Then this site is the one you want to visit. I've set up a way for people to work with me in a more "formal" arrangement that can be mutually beneficial.

SellDomainsForProfit.com

If you reserve more than 50 or 60 domain names a year, then you need to check this site out. You'll save yourself a ton of money doing it this way.

TheSpeakingSchool.com

Want to learn how to speak like a pro? This is the site to visit to learn how to become a more "natural" speaker. Just 6 people max can attend this event.

PublishingSeminar.com

This yearly event geared to authors and publishers is recorded each year. You'll learn all the tips and techniques needed to make more money publishing books and other products.

Someone You Should Meet

(Please note that at many of these sites I receive an affiliate commission if you buy anything. This will not affect your purchase price and I would never recommend anything just to get paid!)

David Hamilton

David is the WebMarketingMagician. He is the person you want to turn to when you have technical questions and problems. Dave will help get your problems solved fast without burning a hole in your wallet.

WebMarketingMagician.com

Other Sites You Should Visit

CoolVideoTool.com

Want to send emails that have maximum impact? Then you need to check out this site. You'll be able to send emails that get people to take action and do what you recommend. This is a future trend you can't ignore.

CoolWordPressTheme.com

Want to make your WordPress site look super good and professional? This site will give you the tools to make it happen. After you do it, you won't believe the difference.

CoolSpyTool.com

Want to SPY on your competition? This is where you need to go to find out exactly what they are doing and how you can turn things to your advantage.

CoolStorageTool.com

Where should you host your audios and videos that you create? Not on YouTube if you want to keep them protected. Check out this site to help you out.

CoolMembershipTool.com

Want to set up a simple membership site? This is the tool you need. You don't need to be a techie to protect your content in a way that virtually anyone can do.

CoolScreenCaptureTool.com

This great tool will allow you to record and capture what you have on your computer screen. It's the best one I've found for doing this. It's simple and easy to use. ALL of my own screen capture videos were done using this software.

If you want to keep up with the latest and greatest ideas and concepts in the field of information marketing, then make sure and sign up for my list and go to my blog. Both of them are available by going to FredGleeck.com/blog.

FREE OFFER

Find out more about the author
by visiting FredGleeck.com

AND to get your FREE
Information Marketing
Audio Course
(worth $397),
go to http://goo.gl/VeClB

FREE OFFER